EVERYDAY WICCA

EVERYDAY
WICCA

Gerina Dunwich

BⒺXTREE

First published 1997 as *The Wicca Book of Days* by Citadel Press, New Jersey

First published in Great Britain 1998 by Boxtree
an imprint of Macmillan Publishers Ltd
25 Eccleston Place, London SW1W 9NF
and Basingstoke

Associated companies throughout the world

ISBN 0 7522 2108 6

1 3 5 7 9 8 6 4 2

A CIP catalogue record for this book is available from
the British Library

Phototypeset by Intype London Ltd
Printed and bound in Great Britain by
Mackays of Chatham plc, Chatham, Kent

To my Mother and to Al B. Jackter (my Gemini soul mate),
I dedicate this book with an abundance of loving gratitude.
Goddess bless you both for all you have done and for always being
there for me.

THE WICCAN WHEEL
OF DAYS

The sacred Wiccan Wheel of Days
is magickal with ancient ways.
Throughout the solar year it turns;
we celebrate, we grow, we learn.

With every moon and every morn
the Pagan magick is reborn,
and like a Witches' circle cast
the power of the Wheel is vast.

With every fleeting minute and hour
the Goddess weaves Her web of power,
guiding us into Her light
where love is the law
and sacred is life.

Magickal with ancient ways
is the Wiccan Wheel of Days,
and as the fires of time do burn
forever shall the Great Wheel turn.

by Gerina Dunwich

CONTENTS

JANUARY

JANUARY, the first month of the current Gregorian calendar and the second month of Winter's rule, derives its name from the ancient Roman god Janus.

The traditional birthstone amulet of January is the garnet; and the carnation and the snowdrop are the month's traditional flowers.

January is shared by the astrological signs of Capricorn the Goat and Aquarius the Water-Bearer, and is sacred to the following Pagan deities: Antu, Felicitas, Inanna, Irene, Janus, Pax, and Venus.

JANUARY 1
New Year's Day

This day is sacred to the goddesses known as the Three Fates, the German goddess Bertha, the Morrigan, the Parcae, and the Japanese household gods.

Many modern Witches and Wiccans around the world traditionally start off the new year with a spell for good luck and a ritual to bless the new year with peace, love, health, and prosperity for all.

This is a traditional time for ending bad habits and beginning New Year resolutions.

The first day of January was dedicated by the ancient Romans to the god Janus (whom the month is named after). Janus possesses two identical faces looking in opposite directions: one to the past, and the other to the future. He is a god of gates and doorways, and a deity associated with journeys and the beginning of things.

Janus
Bronze Roman coin
from about 350 B.C.

JANUARY 2

The birth of the Pagan goddess Inanna has been celebrated annually on this date since ancient times. Inanna is the Sumerian queen of heaven and earth, and a deity who presides over both love and war.

Every year on this date, the Perihelion of the Earth takes place. When this occurs, the planet Earth reaches the point in its orbit closest to the Sun. Many astrologers consider this to be a highly significant event.

In ancient Egypt, a religious ceremony known as the Advent of Isis from Phoenecia was performed yearly on this date in honor of the goddess Isis.

JANUARY 3

On this day, an annual fertility ceremony known as the Deer Dances is performed by the Native American tribe of the Pueblo in the southwestern United States. The ceremony, which includes sacred ritual dances performed by shamans wearing deer headdresses, is centuries-old and dedicated to the great female spirit-goddesses known as the Deer Mothers.

In ancient Greece, a Pagan religious festival called the *Lenaia* was celebrated each year on this date in honor of Dionysus, the god of wine and fertility.

JANUARY 4

In Korea, the annual Sacrifice to the Seven Stars (*Chilseong-je*) is performed on this date at midnight. To receive good fortune and divine blessings, water and white rice are offered to the god who rules the constellation Ursa Major.

JANUARY 5

Twelfth Night and Wassail Eve (in England) heralds the end of Christmastide.

In ancient Egyptian times, it was believed that the waters of the mystical and sacred River Nile possessed special magickal powers on this date.

On this date in the year 1918, renowned astrologer and author Jeane Dixon was born in Medford, Wisconsin.

JANUARY 6
Day of the Triple Goddess

On this date in the year 1988, Circle Sanctuary of Mount Horeb, Wisconsin, became legally recognized as a Wiccan Church by its local Township and County levels of government. Circle Sanctuary's attainment of church zoning was a significant victory for Wiccans around the world, for it was the first time a Witchcraft group had been publicly sanctioned as a church by local government officials.

JANUARY 7

In the seventeenth century, it was customary on this day for a special Epiphany Cake to be baked with a coin in it. Whoever was lucky enough to receive the portion containing the coin was saluted by the family as a "king" or "queen" for the day. As part of the tradition, the "king" or "queen" would draw cross symbols on the ceiling with white chalk to drive out evil spirits and ward off misfortune.

JANUARY 8
Old Druid's New Year

In ancient Greece, Midwife's Day (dedicated to the goddess Babo) was celebrated annually on this date, while an annual festival called Justicia's Day was celebrated by the early Romans.

In ancient times, this day was dedicated to the Norse goddess Freya (or Freyja), who presided over both love and fertility.

JANUARY 9

On this date in the year 1989, Jamie Dodge (a Wiccan who had been fired from her job at the Salvation Army because of

her Wiccan beliefs) won a lawsuit against her former employer
for violating her First Amendment right to freedom of religion
and unnecessary entanglement of government with religion.

On this date in the year 1880, "Old Dorothy" Clutterbuck
was born in Bengal. She belonged to a hereditary Witch coven
in the New Forest of England, and was the High Priestess who
initiated Gerald B. Gardner into the Craft in 1939. She passed
away in the year 1951.

JANUARY 10

The Feast of Dreams, a centuries-old ritual, is performed annually by the Native American Indian tribe of the Iroquois to
celebrate their New Year, which occurs on this date.

In rural England and Scotland, Plough Monday (the first
Monday after Epiphany) occurs on or around this date. A
plough is traditionally paraded through the streets and a ritual
sweeping with brooms is performed to drive away evil spirits
from the village.

JANUARY 11

In years gone by, an old ritual to ward off Witches was performed annually on this date in many fishing villages along
the coast of Scotland. At sunset, a barrel of tar would be
placed on top of a pole, set on fire, and allowed to burn
throughout the night. Afterwards, charred pieces of it would
then be used by the villagers and fishermen as protective
charms.

In ancient Rome, a festival called the *Carmentalia* was celebrated annually, beginning on this date and lasting until the
fifteenth of January. The festival honored the Roman goddess
Carmenta, a deity presiding over childbirth, whose priestesses
cast the fortunes of children at the moment of their birth.

Juturna, the ancient Italian goddess of pools and still
waters, is honored each year on this day.

JANUARY 12

Each year on this date, a sacred solstice ritual called the *Makara-Sankranti* is celebrated by Hindus in India with saffron, songs of joy, and ritual baths in sacred rivers.

JANUARY 13

Saint Silvester's Day. Evil spirits are traditionally driven away with clanging bells on this night by villagers in Urnasch, Switzerland, where the pre-Julian New Year's Eve continues to be celebrated on this date.

In pre-Christian Ireland, the thirteenth day of January was celebrated each year as the Feast of Brewing by the ancient and mysterious priests known as the Druids.

JANUARY 14

On this date in the year 1967, a psychedelic spiritual "pow-wow" called the Human Be-In took place in San Francisco's Golden Gate Park. The event drew approximately 20,000 people (including Allen Ginsberg and Timothy Leary) and consisted of chanting, dancing, poetry readings, music, and celebrations of love and the unity of humankind.

In Southern India, the three-day *Pongal* festival begins on this date each year to celebrate the January rice harvest, honor the great sun-god Surya, and give thanks to the spirits who bring the rainy season.

JANUARY 15

In ancient Rome, a sacred festival called the Feast of the Ass was celebrated each year on this date in honor of the goddess Vesta and the ass that saved her. Vesta presided over the hearth and her temple was lit by a sacred fire tended by six virgin priestesses known as the Vestal Virgins.

JANUARY 16

Each year on this date in the country of Indonesia, the fire-god Betoro Bromo is honored by Buddhist monks and pilgrims who gather at Mount Bromo. At the first stroke of midnight, offerings of food and flowers are cast into the volcano where the god is believed to dwell.

On this date in the year 1976, the famous astrologer and author known as Zolar died.

JANUARY 17

Wassailing the Apple Trees, a ritual dating back to old Celtic Britain, is held annually on this date (the eve of the old Twelfth Night). A traditional libation of cider is poured on the roots of apple trees while an old invocation is sung to the tree in order to ensure fertility and to drive away all evil-natured supernatural entities.

JANUARY 18

In the country of China, the kitchen-god *Zao Jun* is honored with prayers and offerings of sweet rice cakes each year on this night, which marks the end of the Chinese year. For luck, paper images of the god are burned and dried beans are thrown onto the roofs of houses.

JANUARY 19

Each year on this date, the *Thorrablottar* (also known as Husband's Day) is celebrated in Iceland. In pre-Christian times, it was celebrated as a Pagan festival in honor of the mighty god Thor, the red-bearded lord of lightning bolts and thunder.

JANUARY 20

On this date (approximately), the Sun enters the astrological sign of Aquarius. Persons born under the sign of the Water

Bearer are said to be inventive, independent, unconventional, and often idealistic. Those born on this day, the cusp of Capricorn and Aquarius, are believed to make the best astrologers. Aquarius is an air sign and is ruled by the planets Saturn and Uranus.

On this date (approximately) in the year 2160, the Age of Aquarius will begin when the Sun moves into the 11th sign of the zodiac. According to many occultists and astrologers, the following two thousand years will be a Golden Age of spiritual enlightenment, mind power, world peace, love, and harmony. However, according to many prophets, the Age of Aquarius will also bring cataclysmic changes in the Earth and its atmosphere.

Aquarius

JANUARY 21

Saint Agnes' Day. On the eve of Saint Agnes' Day, according to ancient legend, an unmarried woman will see her future husband in a dream. Saint Agnes' Day (named after the Roman Catholic child martyr who was beheaded in the year 304 A.D. for refusing to marry) is an ideal time for Witches to cast love spells and prepare love potions and charms.

This day of the year is sacred to Yngona, an ancient goddess worshipped by the Danish people in pre-Christian times.

JANUARY 22

Festival of the Muses. Each year on this date, the invisible spirits that inspire and watch over all poets, musicians, and artists are honored and invoked with Goddess-inspired poetry, Pagan folk songs, music, and dancing.

JANUARY 23

A Pagan festival known as the Day of Hathor is celebrated annually on this date in Egypt to honor the ancient cow-headed goddess of heaven, beauty, and love. A libation of cow's milk is poured into the River Nile as prayers to the goddess are recited.

JANUARY 24

Ekeko, the Aymara Indian pot-bellied god of prosperity, is honored on this date with an annual fair called the *Alacitas*, which is held in La Paz, Bolivia.

In Hungary, a Pagan purification ceremony known as the Blessing of the Candle of the Happy Women is performed annually on this date.

JANUARY 25

Good-luck rituals are traditionally performed during the Vietnamese Lunar New Year Festival (*Tet*), which takes place annually on or around this date. Offerings are made to ancient deities and ancestors, traditional feasts are prepared, and evil spirits are driven away with whistles, bells, and horns.

JANUARY 26

Each year on the second new moon after the winter solstice (which normally occurs on or around this time of the month), the traditional Chinese New Year begins and is celebrated for two consecutive weeks until the full moon. On the first day of the New Year, ancestral spirits are honored and houses are decorated with strips of red paper to attract good luck and ward off evil ghosts. A Lantern Festival and Dragon Parade traditionally take place on the last night of the New Year celebration.

JANUARY 27

On this date, the annual Day of Ishtar ceremony takes place to honor the ancient Assyrian/Babylonian goddess of love, fertility, and battle. Ishtar is identified with the ancient Phoenician goddess called Astarte.

JANUARY 28

In the Shetland Islands, a centuries-old fire festival known as *Up-Helly-Aa* is held each year on the last Tuesday of January (which normally falls around this date). The festival, which marks the end of the traditional Yuletide and pays tribute to the old gods and goddesses of the ancient Viking religion, climaxes with the torching of a replica of a Viking ship. The day ends with a traditional prayer to drive away evil entities from village homes.

JANUARY 29

On this day in the year 1688, famous mystic, scientist, and spiritualist-medium Emanuel Swedenborg was born in Sweden. His works had a major influence upon the secret societies of the eighteenth century, and a religion based on his mystical theological philosophy was founded in his name by his followers.

In the country of Vietnam, a mystical and centuries-old Parade of the Unicorns takes place each year on this date (approximately).

According to mythology, the ancient Pagan goddesses Irene and Pax were born on this day.

JANUARY 30

In ancient Rome, an agricultural festival called the *Feriae Sementiva* (Feast of Spring) was celebrated annually on this date with sacrifices to Ceres (the goddess of agriculture) and Tellus Mater (the goddess of the Earth and fertility), as well as other lesser gods and goddesses associated with agriculture.

On this date in the year 1940, Z. Budapest (the founder and leader of the main branch of feminist Dianic Wicca) was born in Budapest. Among her many accomplishments, she founded the Susan B. Anthony Coven (named after the

Ceres

famous suffragist), hosted a radio show in San Francisco, directed the Women's Spirituality Forum in Oakland, and led a successful public hexing against a mass murderer.

JANUARY 31

Each year on or around this date, a sacred festival is held in the Katmandu Valley of Nepal in honor of the goddess Sarasvati, an ancient Indian deity who presides over all forms of education. At temples dedicated to her, offerings of food, flowers, and incense are made by faithful Hindus and students who seek her help on their school exams. In the courtyard of the Hanuman Dhoka, an ancient palace where the king is accompanied on this day by Nepalese officials, the annual rites of Spring begin with a traditional gun salute, followed by veneration ceremonies which are performed by the royal priest.

In the Hawaiian Islands, a joyous flower-filled festival in honor of an ancient goddess associated with the narcissus flower is celebrated each year on this day; while in China, an annual festival honoring Kuan Yin takes place.

FEBRUARY

FEBRUARY, the second month of the current Gregorian calendar and the third month of Winter's rule, derives its name from *Februa,* the name of a Roman purification festival held on the fifteenth day of February in ancient times.

The traditional birthstone amulet of February is the amethyst; and the primrose and the violet are the month's traditional flowers.

February is shared by the astrological signs of Aquarius the Water-Bearer and Pisces the Two Fishes, and is sacred to the following Pagan deities: Aradia, Brigid, Juno Februa, and the Wiccan Goddess in Her aspect as the Maiden.

During the month of February, the Great Solar Wheel of the Year is turned to Candlemas, one of the four Grand Sabbats celebrated each year by Wiccans and modern Witches throughout the world.

FEBRUARY 1
Candlemas Eve

Brigit, the Celtic Earth-Mother and goddess of fire, wisdom, poetry, and sacred wells, is honored on this day. In Ireland, offerings of yellow flowers are made to the goddess at sacred wells dedicated to her.

In ancient Greece, the three-day Lesser Eleusinian Mysteries began each year on this day in honor of the goddesses Ceres, Demeter, Persephone, and Proserpine.

FEBRUARY 2

On this day, the Candlemas Sabbat is celebrated by Wiccan and Witches throughout the world. Candlemas (which is also known as Imbolc, Oimelc, and Lady Day) is a fire festival that celebrates the coming of Spring. New beginnings and spiritual growth are represented by the "sweeping out of the old," symbolized by the sweeping of the circle with a besom (a Witch's broom). This is traditionally done by the High Priestess of the coven, who wears a brilliant crown of thirteen candles on top of her head. In ancient Europe, the Candlemas Sabbat was celebrated with a torchlight procession to purify and fertilize the fields before the seed-planting season, and to honor and give thanks to the various deities and spirits associated with agriculture.

FEBRUARY 3

On this date, an annual ceremony called the Blessing of the Throats takes place to honor the healing powers of Saint Blaise and to magickally ward off throat ailments brought on by the winter's cold.

FEBRUARY 4

Throughout Japan the evil demons of winter are exorcised annually on this day with a festival called the *Setsubun*.

Beans are placed in every corner of a family's house, and pointed branches and sardine heads are mounted over the doors. Centuries-old purification rites are performed by priests in all temples and shrines. Prayers are written on slips of paper and then cast from bridges into the rivers below.

FEBRUARY 5

On this date in the year 1962, the Great Conjunction of the Sun, Moon, Venus, Mars, Mercury, Jupiter, and Saturn occurred in the sign of Aquarius.

On this day, the annual Feast of Ia is celebrated in honor of, and to invoke the powers of, the Sacred Maiden of the Pagan mythos.

FEBRUARY 6

Throughout northern Japan, a centuries-old winter snow festival takes place each year around this time of the month. The ancient and beneficial spirits that bring life-sustaining water are honored at special shrines erected in huts resembling Eskimo igloos.

A festival in honor of the love goddess Aphrodite was held each year on this date in ancient Greece.

FEBRUARY 7

On this date (approximately), the annual spring fertility festival known as Li Chum is celebrated in China. Bamboo and paper effigies of a water buffalo (an animal which symbolizes "new life") are carried through the streets by a temple bound procession. After reaching the temple, the effigies are set on fire in the belief that prayers for prosperity will be taken up to heaven by the rising smoke.

FEBRUARY 8

The annual nighttime ritual known as the Star Festival is celebrated on this date (approximately) in China. The stars that influence the fate of mankind are honored by the lighting of 108 small lanterns on a special altar, and prayers are offered to the sacred stars that governed one's birth.

FEBRUARY 9

In northern Norway, the Narvik Sun Pageant is held annually on this date in honor of the ancient Pagan goddess who rules over the Sun. The festival, which has been celebrated since pre-Christian times, begins at sunrise and continues throughout the day until the shadows of evening darken the sky.

FEBRUARY 10

An ancient African festival marking the beginning of the fishing season and the New Year is celebrated annually on this day by members of the Kebbawa tribe of Nigeria. The ancient gods of their religion are honored and invoked, and traditional fish divinations are performed.

In pre-Christian times, the goddess Anaitis was honored on this day in the country of Persia (now Iran). She was a deity who was said to have possessed great powers over the Moon and the seas.

FEBRUARY 11

Each year on this date, millions of faithful men, women, and children make a pilgrimage to the shrine of Our Lady in Lourdes. A spring in the village of Lourdes, France, is believed by many to possess curative powers. The pilgrims bathe in the water in the hope that it will heal their illnesses and disabilities.

FEBRUARY 12

On this date in the year 1663, the infamous clergyman Cotton Mather was born in Boston, Massachusetts. (This is certainly one birthday no Witch would ever celebrate!) His writings and sermons condemning the practice of the Old Religion contributed greatly to the hysteria of the 1692 Salem Witch-hunt. Cotton Mather died in Boston, one day after his birthday, in the year 1728.

FEBRUARY 13

On this date, an annual holiday called the *Parentalia* was observed in ancient Rome. It lasted until the twenty-first of February and was a day for families to honor and commemorate their deceased loved ones, particularly their parents. During the week of *Parentalia,* all temples in Rome were closed and all wedding ceremonies forbidden. Ancestral tombs were visited and offerings of wine and flowers were made to family ghosts.

FEBRUARY 14

Saint Valentine's Day. This is a day dedicated to all lovers, and the traditional time for Witches around the world to practice all forms of love magick and love divination.

This day is sacred to Juno-Lupa, the she-wolf goddess of the ancient Roman religion. In early times, she was honored annually on this day by a women's fertility festival and the sacrifice of a female wolf.

FEBRUARY 15

On this date in ancient Rome, a festival known as the Lupercalia (Feast of the Wolf) was celebrated to honor the god

The Wonders of the Invisible World.

OBSERVATIONS

As well *Historical* as *Theological*, upon the NATURE, the NUMBER, and the OPERATIONS of the

DEVILS.

Accompany'd with,

I. Some Accounts of the Grievous Molestations, by DÆ-MONS and WITCHCRAFTS, which have lately annoy'd the Countrey; and the Trials of some eminent *Malefactors* Executed upon occasion thereof: with several Remarkable *Curiosities* therein occurring.

II. Some Counsils, Directing a due Improvement of the terrible things, lately done, by the Unusual & Amazing Range of EVIL SPIRITS, in Our Neighbourhood: & the methods to prevent the *Wrongs* which those *Evil Angels* may intend against all sorts of people among us, especially in Accusations of the Innocent.

III. Some Conjectures upon the great EVENTS, likely to befall, the WORLD in General, and NEW ENGLAND in Particular; as also upon the Advances of the TIME, when we shall see BETTER DAYES.

IV. A short Narrative of a late Outrage committed by a knot of WITCHES in *Swedeland*, very much Resembling, and so far Explaining, *That* under which our parts of *America* have laboured !

V. THE DEVIL DISCOVERED: In a Brief Discourse upon those TEMPTATIONS, which are the more Ordinary *Devices* of the Wicked One.

By **Cotton Mather.**

Boston Printed by *Benj. Harris* for *Sam. Phillips.* 1693.

Title page of witch-hunt pamphlet by Cotton Mather

Lupercus and to mark the beginning of Spring. The festival, which was a rustic ritual of both purification and fertility magick, also included the sacrifice of goats and dogs to the god Faunus (identified by classical writers as the horned goat-god

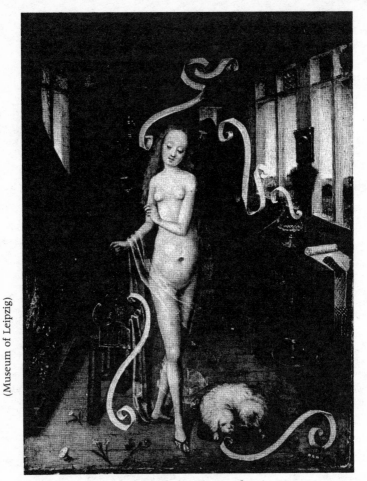

The Witch by G. D. Platzi
Sixteenth century

Pan). During the orgiastic festival, young men would choose their sexual partners by drawing the names of young women out of a bowl.

FEBRUARY 16

In the distant past, a rite called the Devil's Dance was performed annually on this date (approximately) as part of the

Tibetan New Year festival. Monks wearing grotesque masks would dance for hours as a village sorcerer exorcised demons and the evil influences of the past year with various magickal incantations.

FEBRUARY 17

On this day, according to Hindu religion and mythology, the fearsome goddess known as Kali was born and the world entered into the Kali Yuga (the "Evil Age"). Kali, the destroyer-goddess, was depicted with black skin, a hideous face, and four arms. In ancient times, human sacrifices were made to appease her and to satisfy her thirst for blood.

FEBRUARY 18

On this day, a festival of women known as the *Spenta Armaiti* was held annually throughout the country of Persia. Ancient fertility rites were performed by temple priestesses in honor of the goddess Spandarmat, and the goddess who dwells within all women was honored and invoked with special prayers and meditations.

FEBRUARY 19

On this date (approximately), the Sun enters the astrological sign of Pisces. Persons born under the sign of the Two Fishes are said to be telepathic, tolerant, sensitive, artistic, and often prone to daydreaming. Pisces is a water sign and is ruled by the planet Neptune.

According to mythology, the goddess Minerva was born on this day (which is sacred to the Pagan deities Nammu and Nina).

Pisces

FEBRUARY 20

On this date in the year 1882, the Society for Psychical Research was founded in London, England, by a group of prominent philosophers and physicists. It became Britain's leading organization for research into the world of supernatural phenomena and the paranormal.

FEBRUARY 21

In ancient Rome, an All Soul's Day ceremony known as the *Feralia* was held annually on this date at the close of the *Parentalia* festival. Family reunions were held and *Lares* (ancestral guardian spirits) were honored with prayers and offerings.

FEBRUARY 22

On this day in the year 1917, Sybil Leek was born in Stoke-on-Trent, England. She achieved fame and success as a modern Witch, astrologer, and occult author. Her psychic predictions of the Kennedy assassinations and the election of Richard M. Nixon as President of the United States are documented. She passed away on October 26, 1982, in Melbourne, Florida.

FEBRUARY 23

On this date, the last festival of the ancient Roman year (the *Terminalia*) was celebrated annually in honor of the god *Terminus*, a deity who ruled over boundaries and frontiers. During the Terminalia, neighbors whose lands were divided and protected by Terminus would gather together and pour libations of wine, honey, and the blood of sacrificed pigs on their stone boundary-markers.

FEBRUARY 24

Shiva, the multifaceted Hindu god of destruction and renewal, is honored annually on this date (approximately) by a day of fasting, followed by an oil-lamp vigil known as the *Shivaratri* (Shiva's Night) which takes place at shrines dedicated to him.

FEBRUARY 25

In many parts of the Christian world, a joyous pre-Lenten celebration known as Carnival takes place annually on or around this date. In ancient days, orgiastic fertility rites and sacrifices of humans and animals to herald the arrival of Spring were common at this time of the year in many parts of the world.

FEBRUARY 26

Pentagram Night. As a symbolic gesture to reaffirm your dedication to the Craft of the Wise, dip your fingertip into a small cauldron pot filled with Yule-log ashes and then use it to draw the sacred symbol of the Witches' Pentagram (five-pointed star within a circle) over your heart at the first stroke of midnight.

FEBRUARY 27

On this day in the year 1861, famous psychic and spiritual philosopher Rudolf Steiner was born in Kraljevic (which was part of Hungary at that time). He possessed clairvoyant powers and communicated often with nonphysical entities. In 1902, he was appointed general secretary of the German Section of the Theosophical Society, and in 1913, he established his own school for esoteric research. He died on March 30, 1925.

FEBRUARY 28

In ancient times, a Chaldean Sabbat known as the *Sabbatu* was celebrated each year on this date.

On this day of the year, the Earth-Goddesses Ceres, Demeter, Gaia, Ge, and Mauri are honored by many Pagans and Wiccans around the world.

Also honored annually on this day is the ancient Pagan deity Zamyaz, who was worshipped and offered sacrifices by the ancient Chaldeans and Persians.

FEBRUARY 29

On this date in the year 1692, Abigail Williams and Ann Putnam, two young girls from Salem Village, Massachusetts, accused three local women of using the black arts of Witchcraft to torment and bewitch them. On the following day, Sarah Good, Sarah Osburne, and a West African slave named Tituba were arrested, marking the beginning of the infamous Salem Witch Trials of 1692. By the end of the year, when the trials were finally brought to a close, over 200 women and men had been arrested and jailed, 19 had been hanged at Gallows Hill, and one man had been pressed to death.

According to folklore, this is a very unlucky day to have a love letter postmarked. It will lead to the breakup of your love affair or engagement.

MARCH

MARCH, the third month of the current Gregorian calendar and the first month of Spring, derives its name from the ancient Roman war-god Mars, who also presided over the fertility of the land.

The traditional birthstone amulets of March are the aquamarine and the bloodstone; and the daffodil and the jonquil are the month's traditional flowers.

March is shared by the astrological signs of Pisces the Two Fishes and Aries the Ram, and is sacred to the following Pagan deities: Eostre, the Green Goddess, the Lord of the Greenwood, Mars, and Ostara.

During the month of March, the Great Solar Wheel of the Year is turned to the Vernal Equinox, one of the four Lesser Sabbats celebrated each year by Wiccans and modern Witches throughout the world.

MARCH 1

On this date in the year 1888, the Hermetic Order of
the Golden Dawn (an influential Western occult order and
secret society) was established. It offered teachings on
ceremonial magick, divination, Kabbalah, and other occult-
oriented sciences. Many of its rituals are still in use by
modern-day practitioners of High Magick. Aleister Crowley
(one of the Golden Dawn's most famous members) was
initiated into the Order in the year 1898 but was later
expelled.

In ancient Rome, the sacred fire in the Temple of Vesta
was rekindled by the Vestal Virgins on this day which, at one
time, marked the beginning of the Roman year.

The first day of March is celebrated in Bulgaria as Granny
March's Day. (Granny March is an old Witch-Goddess who
presides over the month of March.) It is believed throughout
the country that if any woman works on this sacred day,
Granny March becomes angry and uses her magickal powers
to destroy the crops with storms.

MARCH 2

In various parts of Europe, women celebrate Mother March
each year on this date. The Mother-Goddess who presides
over the third month of the year is honored and a festive
parade is held to commemorate all women who have created
life.

MARCH 3

The number three is the most magickal of all numbers;
therefore, the third day of the third month is believed to be a
favorable time for Witches and practitioners of magick
throughout the world.

This day is sacred to all Triple Goddesses and deities of

the Moon (which shows itself in three aspects: waxing, full, and waning). The magickal and healing power of pyramids is said to be strongest on this day.

MARCH 4

On this day in Ireland and Wales, the annual Feast of Rhiannon is celebrated by many Wiccans in honor of Rhiannon, the Celtic/ Welsh Mother Goddess who was originally known as Rigatona (the Great Queen) and identified with the Gaulish mare-goddess Epona.

On this date in ancient Greece, an annual ritual called the *Anthesteria* was held to honor the souls of the dead (the *Keres*). The ritual lasted for three days.

On this date in the year 1968, the Church of All Worlds (founded by Otter Zell) was formally chartered, thus becoming the first federally recognized church of Neo-Paganism.

MARCH 5

In parts of North Africa, the ancient Egyptian goddess Isis is honored on this date with an annual festival of music, dancing, and feasting. In Rome, Isis's opening of the seas to navigation was commemorated on this day with an annual ceremony called the *Navigum Isidis* (Blessing of the Vessel of Isis).

MARCH 6

According to an ancient book called *Perillous Dayes of Every Month*, the sixth and seventh days of March "shall come to no good end, and the dayes be full perillous for many things."

On this date (approximately) in the year 1795, Count Alessandro Cagliostro died in prison. He was renowned as an alchemist, healer, psychic, and practitioner of wizardry before falling victim to the Catholic Church's Inquisition.

MARCH 7

On this day in the year 1890, the poet William Butler Yeats was initiated into the Isis-Urania Temple of the Hermetic Order of the Golden Dawn. There, he studied the magickal arts and took the magickal name *Daemon est Deus Inversus* (which translates into "The Devil is God Reversed").

MARCH 8

Mother Earth Day, a festival which honors the birthday of the Earth as a Mother Goddess, is celebrated annually on this day throughout China. The festival consists of street parades, the lighting of firecrackers, feasting and partying. "Birthday presents" (coins, flowers, incense, paper dolls, etc.) are placed in small holes in the ground, blessed, and then covered with soil.

MARCH 9

On this date, the annual Butter Lamp Festival is held by Buddhist monks in Tibet to render demons powerless and to secure the favor of the gods. Yak-butter sculptures of Buddhist heroes are paraded through the streets as sacred chants are recited. After the procession, the sculptures are then cast into the waters of a river.

MARCH 10

On this day in the year 1909, the famous Dutch clairvoyant and psychic healer Gerard Croiset was born in the Netherlands. Using his clairvoyant abilities, which manifested early in his childhood, Croiset healed hundreds of patients daily at his clinic. He also worked with various police departments as a psychic criminologist and solved crimes in more than half a dozen countries. His death occurred on July 20, 1980.

MARCH 11

Jacques de Molay, the last Grand Master of the Order of the Knights Templars, was burned alive at the stake on this date in the year 1314. Shortly before he died, he accurately predicted the death of King Philip IV of France within the year and the death of Pope Clement V within forty days.

MARCH 12
Babylonian Feast of Marduk

On this day in the year 1873, psychic researcher and occultist Stewart Edward White was born in Grand Rapids, Michigan. He authored several books containing material obtained through his wife's spirit-channeling sessions, and he served as president of the American Society for Psychical Research in San Francisco, California.

MARCH 13

The thirteenth day of the third month is considered to be the luckiest day of the year for all Witches (especially if it should happen to fall on a Friday), as thirteen is the number associated with the traditional Witches' coven and three is a powerful magickal number.

In Luxemborg, a Pagan fire festival known as *Burgsonndeg* is celebrated annually on this day with the lighting of great bonfires to welcome Spring and the rebirth of the Sun.

MARCH 14

The annual thirteen-day Ghanian New Year celebration begins on this date. A series of special ritual dances are traditionally performed on the first eleven days of the festival to dispel all evil spirits and honor the souls of the departed. The shrines of the beneficial spirits are ritually purified on the twelfth day, and a joyous celebration of the new year takes place on the thirteenth day.

This day is sacred to Ua Zit, a serpent-goddess of the ancient Egyptian religion.

MARCH 15

On this date in ancient Rome, the annual Festival of Attis and Cybele began with a procession of reed-bearers to commemorate the finding of the infant Attis among the reeds. The festival was followed by nine consecutive days of fasting and sexual abstinence.

MARCH 16

The annual Hindu festival of *Holi* is held in India on this date to celebrate Spring and to commemorate the burning death of the child-eating, she-demon known as Holika.

On this date in the year 1946, J. Z. Knight, the famous spirit channeler for the ancient entity known as "Ramtha," was born in New Mexico.

MARCH 17
Saint Patrick's Day

On this date in the year 1893, Eileen J. Garrett (a gifted medium, psychic, and founder of the Parapsychology Foundation) was born in Ireland. At a young age, she began experiencing visions of the dead. She was granted United States citizenship in 1947 and she founded her own publishing house (Creative Age Press) and magazine (*Tomorrow*, a journal of paranormal phenomena). She established the Parapsychology Foundation in 1951, and wrote numerous books under the pen name of Jean Lyttle. She died in France on September 15, 1970.

MARCH 18

In ancient times, the Pagan fertility-goddess known as Sheela-na-gig was honored annually on this date in Ireland. With the advent of Christianity, the identity of the goddess was altered from heathen deity with oversized genitalia to the consort or mother of Saint Patrick.

On this day in the year 1877, psychic and "absent healer" Edgar Cayce (also known as the Sleeping Prophet) was born in Hopkinsville, Kentucky. He was renowned for his psychic visions and miraculous ability to accurately diagnose illnesses and prescribe remedies while in a self-induced trance. He prophesied the Second Coming of Christ in the year 1998, followed by cataclysmic changes of the planet. Edgar Cayce died on January 3, 1945.

MARCH 19

The *Akitu*, an annual Babylonian New Year festival celebrating the marriage of Heaven and Earth, begins on this date and lasts for ten consecutive days.

In ancient times, Greek theatrical performances known as the *Urban Dionysia* began annually on this date in honor of the god Dionysus. They continued for five consecutive days. Also, a festival called the *Lesser Panathenaea* was held at this time. It was dedicated to the goddess Athena.

Sitala, a goddess who reigns over smallpox and death, is honored on this day in India as part of the Hindu New Year ritual.

MARCH 20
Rosicrucian New Year

On this date, an annual Spring Harvest Festival was celebrated in ancient Egypt, along the banks of the River Nile, in honor of the Mother-Goddess and the enchantress Isis.

This day is sacred to the goddess Fortuna, the Morrigan, the Norns, the Three Fates, and the Three Mothers (Lakshmi, Parvati, and Sarasvati).

MARCH 21

On this date (approximately), the Sun enters the astrological sign of Aries. Persons born under the sign of the Ram are said to be courageous, intelligent, impulsive, and aggressive. Aries is a fire sign and is ruled by the planet Mars.

Aries

MARCH 22

On the first day of Spring (which normally occurs on or near this date) the Spring, or Vernal, Equinox is celebrated by Wiccans and Witches throughout the world. Spring Equinox (which is also known as Festival of the Trees, Alban Eilir, O tara, and the Rite of Eostre) is a fertility rite celebrating the birth of Spring and the reawakening of life from the Earth. On this sacred day, Witches light new fires at sunrise, rejoice, ring bells, and decorate hardboiled eggs—an ancient Pagan custom associated with the Goddess of Fertility. The aspects of the Goddess invoked at this Sabbat are Eostre (the Saxon goddess of fertility) and Ostara (the German goddess of fertility); in some Wiccan traditions, the Green Goddess and the Lord of the Greenwood are worshipped on this day. Like most of the old Pagan festivals, Spring Equinox was Christianized by the Church into the religious holiday of Easter, which celebrates the resurrection of Jesus Christ.

On this date in ancient Rome, uprooted pine trees were carried through the streets of the city by the devotees of the cult of Attis and taken to his sacred temple as part of an annual ritual (Procession of the Tree-Bearers) to mourn the god's demise.

MARCH 23

Dance of the Salii. On this date in ancient Rome, the gods Mars and Saturn were invoked each year by dancing priests brandishing spears and clashing holy shields. The evil spirits of Winter were thus expelled from the city, and the growth of crops and gardens was stimulated through sympathetic magick.

In the Polish countryside, an old Pagan festival of Spring called the *Marzenna* is celebrated annually on this date with singing, dancing, and the "sacrifices" of straw effigies.

MARCH 24

Day of Blood. In ancient Rome this was a time of deep mourning. It was an annual religious custom on this day for people to lacerate themselves with knives and for new priests to castrate themselves and spill their blood on the altar in the temple of the Mother-Goddess Cybele.

MARCH 25

The *Hilaria* (Festival of Joy) was celebrated annually on this date in ancient Rome. It was a joyous event which commemorated the triumph of day over night after the Vernal Equinox. The festivities were brought to a close with a "ceremony of washing" which was believed to promote fertility.

MARCH 26

Solitude Day. This is a time for Wiccans and Neo-Pagans to spend the day (or at least part of it) by themselves, meditate in solitude, and reconnect with their "inner selves." Take a quiet walk in the woods or stroll down a deserted beach and listen to the music of the sea. Explore an old barn or write a Goddess-inspired poem.

MARCH 27

In ancient Rome, the fertility and wine-god Liber Pater was honored annually on this date (and sometimes on the seventeenth of March). His festival, the *Liberalia,* was a time of feasting and drinking, and a day when young males entered into their manhood.

Gauri, the goddess of marriage and abundance, is honored on this date in India with an annual women's festival and swinging ritual.

MARCH 28

The *Eka Dasa Rudra* (an eleven-week-long Balinese festival consisting of thirty ceremonies) is held on this date approximately once every one hundred years to restore the balance between the forces of good and evil. The festival, which is ancient in origin, reaches a climax when thousands of pilgrims gather at the volcano temple to observe animal sacrifices made to appease the god Rudra.

In Taiwan, the birthday of the goddess Kwan Yin is celebrated annually on this date.

MARCH 29

The annual Festival of Ishtar is celebrated by many Wiccans on this day in honor of the Assyrian and Babylonian goddess of love, fertility, and battle. As a Triple Goddess, Ishtar represents birth, death, and rebirth.

On this day, an annual masquerade ritual is held by the Bobo people of Africa to restore the balance of Nature and to ward off evil spirits. Special prayers and offerings are made to the gods of rain and the gods of the harvest.

MARCH 30

The annual Iranian New Year celebration begins on this date and continues for thirteen days. Bonfires are lit and sacred rituals involving eggs and mirrors are performed.

A Pagan religious festival was held each year on this day in ancient Mesopotamia to celebrate the sacred union of the God and Goddess, and to give thanks for the creation of the human race.

MARCH 31

On this date in ancient Rome, the annual Feast of Luna was celebrated at moonrise in honor of the beautiful and powerful goddess of the Moon and lunar magick.

On this date in the year 1848, the famous Fox Sisters supposedly made communication with the spirit world at Hydesville Cottage in upstate New York. Their famous seances gave birth to the popular spiritualist movement, which was all the rage in the United States and England from the mid-1880's to the early twentieth century.

APRIL

APRIL, the fourth month of the current Gregorian calendar and the second month of Spring's rule, derives its name from *Aprillis,* the Latin name for the ancient Roman love-goddess Aphrodite. Other reference sources give *aperire,* the Latin word meaning "to open," as the origination of the month's name.

The traditional birthstone amulet of April is the diamond, and the daisy and the sweet pea are the month's traditional flowers.

April is shared by the astrological signs of Aries the Ram and Taurus the Bull, and is sacred to the following Pagan deities: Aphrodite, Artemis, Astarte, Erzulie, Terra, Venus, and Ying-Hua.

APRIL 1

The month of Venus begins with April Fool's Day (also known as All Fools' Day), an occasion for playing practical jokes on friends, family, and coworkers. This custom dates back to olden times, when inmates of insane asylums were allowed out in the streets for one day each year for the sadistic amusement of those who were (supposedly) normal.

APRIL 2

The old Pagan custom of "carrying death away" is carried out in certain regions of Germany on this day. In celebration of Winter's demise, special straw dolls are burned in sacred bonfires or "drowned" in sacred wells.

APRIL 3

In Iran, on the thirteenth day of their New Year, special bowls containing sprouted seeds are traditionally cast into the rivers as offerings in the belief that the bad luck of the previous year will be carried away.

    The goddess Persephone's annual return from the Underworld, allowing the Earth to bloom again, was celebrated every year on this date by the ancient Romans.

APRIL 4

The annual festival of Cybele, the *Megalesia*, was celebrated on this date in ancient Rome. She was a goddess of fertility whose cult originated in Phrygia. Her male attendants were self-castrated priests and worship of her was wild and orgiastic.

APRIL 5

Festival of Kuan Yin. Every year on this day, Kuan Yin (the powerful Chinese goddess of healing, mercy, compassion, and forgiveness) is invoked for protection, love, mercy, and wisdom. Offerings of incense and violet-colored candles are placed on her altar, along with rolled-up pieces of rice paper upon which various wishes have been written.

APRIL 6

In France, a children's springtime festival takes place on this day. Miniature pine boats, each holding a burning candle, are cast into the estuaries of the Moselle River to symbolize the "sea of life" and the happiness of sailing its sacred waves.

APRIL 7

The Blajini (or "kindly ones") are celebrated annually on this day in various parts of Rumania. This is a sacred day in which offerings are made to the beneficent spirits of the water and the Underworld.

APRIL 8

On this date in 1994, a group of Pagans carrying placards, banners, balloons, and streamers paraded joyously in Gainesville, Florida. They praised the Mother Goddess and invited all to celebrate the beauty of life. The focus of this Freedom of Religion Parade (sponsored by the Alachua Pagan Alliance) was to highlight the religious diversity of the community and to help foster tolerance.

APRIL 9

Feast of A-Ma. Once a year on this day, the ancient goddess A-Ma is honored with a religious festival in the Portuguese territory of Macao. A-Ma is the patroness of fisherman and all those who sail the sea.

This day is sacred to all Amazon goddesses.

In England, the Hocktide Festival takes place on this date each year to celebrate the triumph of the Saxon she-warriors who battled against Danish invaders in the year A.D. 1002.

APRIL 10

According to ancient Celtic folklore, the Sun dances each year on this day. In many parts of Ireland, people arise at the first light of dawn to watch the Sun "dance" in a shimmering bowl of water.

Bau, the Goddess Mother of Ea, was honored each year on this day in ancient Babylonia with a sacred religious festival called The Day of Bau.

APRIL 11

On this day each year, cross-inscribed loaves of bread are traditionally baked in honor of the Roman goddess Diana.

In Greece, branches of evergreen, myrtle, or bay were worn by children on this day for protection against the venomous evil eye.

In Armenia, the goddess Anahit is honored annually on this day with a sacred festival. She is a deity of both love and lunar power who dwells within the silver light of the Moon.

APRIL 12

The *Cerealia*, an annual festival of the goddess Ceres, was celebrated by the ancient Romans in order to secure the fertility of the crops. The sacred rites of Ceres began on this date and were observed for eight consecutive days.

In Taiwan, the goddess who presides over birth (Chu-Si-Niu) is honored annually on this day with a religious festival. Pregnant women go to temples dedicated to her in order to receive blessings for their unborn children.

APRIL 13

On this day, an annual festival of water is celebrated by Buddhists in Thailand. Buddha statues are ritually bathed and the water is thrown on the faithful to purify and "wash away" the evil spirits of the previous year. The festival lasts for three consecutive days.

APRIL 14

According to superstitious belief, the fourteenth day of April is a very unlucky time for travel, especially by ship. (It was on this date in the year 1912 that the oceanliner *Titanic* collided with an iceberg and sank to the bottom of the sea.) Whether the *Titanic* tragedy spawned the superstition or merely served to reinforce it is unknown.

Maryamma (or Mariamne), the Hindu goddess of the sea, is honored in India with a sacred festival which begins annually on this day.

APRIL 15

In ancient Rome, the earth-goddess Tellus (or Tellus Mater) was honored annually on this day. A pregnant cow was traditionally sacrificed at her sacred festival and the unborn calf burned in a bonfire to ensure the fertility of the crops.

Also on this day, the Festival of the Iron Phallus (*Kanamara Matsuri*) is celebrated annually in Kawasaki City, Japan. The ancient Japanese deities associated with sexuality and human reproduction give their sacred blessings and encouragement, especially to couples who wed late in life or to men who suffer from declining potency.

APRIL 16

Every year on this day, the god Apollo was worshipped and supplicated by his faithful cult in ancient Greece. An annual festival called the *Hiketeria* was celebrated in his honor.

On this date in the year 1946, Pagan author Margot Adler was born in Little Rock, Arkansas. Her Wiccan hand-fasting on June 19, 1988 was the first Neo-Pagan Wedding to appear in the *New York Times'* society pages.

APRIL 17

In the Himalayan kingdom of Nepal, an annual religious event called the Chariot Festival of the Rain God begins on this day. It is dedicated to Machendrana, the ancient and powerful Indian god of rain. The festival is celebrated for approximately eight consecutive weeks.

APRIL 18

The Festival of Rama-Navami is celebrated every year on this date at sacred shrines throughout India. It honors both the great Hindu god Rama (the seventh incarnation of Vishnu) and the goddess Sita.

APRIL 19

On this date in the year 1824, Lord Byron (whose real name was George Gordon) died of a fever. The English poet, who was known for dabbling in the occult arts, helped shape Mary Shelley's *Frankenstein* and gave John Polidori the idea for his novel *The Vampyre*. Lord Byron's heart was removed from his corpse and buried in Greece; the rest of his remains were shipped back to England.

APRIL 20

On this date (approximately) the Sun enters the astrological sign of Taurus. Persons born under the sign of the Bull are said to be stable, reliable, patient, and often stubborn. Taurus is an earth sign and is ruled by the planet Venus.

Taurus

APRIL 21

Birthday of Rome. On this day, an annual festival called the *Palilia* (Feast of Pales) was celebrated in ancient Rome to honor the pastoral goddess Pales. In the country, special purification rites were performed to keep the sheep disease-free. Shepherds, followed by their flock, would traditionally leap through bonfires. In the city of Rome, the festival was celebrated with wine and merriment.

APRIL 22

Earth Day. This is a day dedicated to Mother Earth and a time for Witches throughout the world to perform Gaia-healing rituals. The first Earth Day took place in 1970 as a result of the Ecology Movement of that time, and since then it has been held each year to help encourage recycling programs and the use of solar energy, and to increase community awareness of important environmental issues.

APRIL 23

The *Vinalia*, a joyous wine festival in honor of the god Jupiter, was held annually on this date in ancient Rome.

On this date in the year 1934, actress Shirley MacLaine was born. Her bestselling spirituality books have had a major influence on the Neo-Pagan movement and have made her name synonymous with the New Age.

On this date in the year 1976, the first national all-woman conference on women's spirituality was held in a rented church in Boston, Massachusetts. Several hundred women attended the event. They proclaimed "The Goddess is alive; magick is afoot!" and invoked Her by dancing, clapping, and chanting. The conference lasted for three consecutive days.

APRIL 24

Saint Mark's Eve. According to folklore of the English countryside, the ghosts of all men, women, and children destined to pass away in the next year can be seen floating by on this night by any person brave enough to spend the night awake on the front porch of a church. However, if a person was unfortunate enough to fall asleep during the vigil or if he failed to repeat it annually for the remainder of his life, he would never wake up the next morning.

APRIL 25

On this date in the year 1989, *USA Today* reported that Patricia Hutchins, a military Wiccan stationed at an air force base in Texas, was granted religious leave by the United States Military in order to observe the eight Sabbats of the Wicca religion. Ms. Hutchins was the first Wiccan in history to have her religious holidays granted by the U.S. Air Force.

APRIL 26

On this New Year's Day in the African republic of Sierra Leone, an ancient seed-sowing ceremony is performed in honor of, and to appease, the powerful goddess of fertility who watches over the crops.

APRIL 27

A mythical half-man, half-animal being called Tyi Wara is honored annually on this date with songs and dance by farmers in the African republic of Mali. It is believed among the Bambara tribe of that region that Tyi Wara was sent down to Earth by the gods of nature in order to teach human beings the necessary skills of farming.

APRIL 28

In ancient Rome, the beautiful goddess Flora was honored annually on this date. She was a fertility and vegetation goddess of Springtime and flowering plants. Her three-day festival, the *Floralia*, marked the beginning of the growing season.

APRIL 29

Pagan Tree Day. On this day, plant a tree dedicated to your favorite Pagan goddess or god. For instance: plant a myrtle tree in honor of Venus and Aphrodite; an oak for Demeter, Diana, and Hera; a pine for Attis, Cybele, and Pan; a rowan tree for all moon-goddesses; a sycamore for all Egyptian gods and goddesses; a willow for Artemis, Brigid, and Persephone; a yew for Hecate and Saturn; etc.

APRIL 30

In Germany, Walpurgisnacht begins at sunrise on this date and ends at sunrise on the first day of May (May Day). Birch boughs are placed on all doors and windows to protect the home from evil spirits and sorcery. Traditional bonfires and torches of rosemary and juniper are lit, and according to legend, Witches can be seen riding across the sky on broomsticks on this dark and magickal night.

On this date in the year 1988, the English Witch Alexander Sanders (also known as King of the Witches) died of lung cancer. He was gifted with psychic powers, and was the founder of the Alexandrian tradition of Wicca.

(Mary Evans Picture Library)

MAY

MAY, the fifth month of the current Gregorian calendar and the third month of Spring's rule, derives its name from the Roman Springtime goddess Maia, whose divine powers encouraged the growth of crops.

The traditional birthstone amulets of May are the emerald and the agate; and the hawthorne and lily are the month's traditional flowers.

May is shared by the astrological signs of Taurus the Bull and Gemini the Twins, and is sacred to the following Pagan deities: Artemis, Diana, Faunus, Flora, Pan, and all gods and goddesses who preside over fertility.

During the month of May, the Great Solar Wheel of the Year is turned to Beltane, one of the four Grand Sabbats celebrated each year by Wiccans and modern Witches throughout the world.

MAY 1

The Beltane Sabbat is celebrated by Wiccans and Witches throughout the world annually on this date. Beltane (which is also known as May Day, Rood Day, Rudemas, and Walpurgisnacht) is derived from an ancient Druid fire festival celebrating the union of the Goddess and the Horned God. It also celebrates the rebirth of the Sun, marking the "death" of Winter and the "birth" of Spring. At dawn, morning dew is gathered from grass and wildflowers to be used in mystical potions for good luck. Throughout the day, Nature is celebrated by feasts, games, poetry readings, and clockwise dancing around a brightly decorated Maypole.

In ancient Rome, the deity worshipped on this day was the Spring goddess Maia, whose divine powers encouraged the crops to grow. The month of May is named after her.

On this date in the year 1776, the Order of the Illuminati (an occult sect and secret order dedicated to the study of forbidden books, Tantric mysticism, and ceremonial magick) was founded in Bavaria by Adam Weishaupt.

MAY 2

On this date, an annual fertility festival featuring a man wearing the costume of a hobbyhorse, a devilish mask, and a pointed hat is held in England and throughout rural regions across Europe.

Ysahodhara, the consort of the great god Buddha, is honored in India with a sacred festival that takes place on this day each year.

MAY 3

In ancient Rome, an annual women's festival in honor of the earth-goddess Bona Dea took place on this date. Sacrifices of sows were made to her in order to promote fertility in women, and the unveiling of sacred objects for only women's eyes to see was included in the celebration of her rites.

MAY 4

Fairy Day. According to Irish folklore, it is on this day that the mischievous fairy folk emerge from their hiding places. To prevent human children from being stolen by the fairies and replaced by grotesque changelings, an offering of tea and bread must be left on the doorstep for the little people. For protection against fairies while traveling (especially through heavily wooded areas or open fields), wear your coat inside out. This is said to cause them such great confusion that they are unable to cause any trouble.

MAY 5

On this date in the year 2000, according to a group called the Lemurian Fellowship, the legendary lost continent of Mu will rise up from the Pacific Ocean.

In various parts of Mexico and Central America, centuries-old rain ceremonies are performed every year on this day by shamanic priests and priestesses of the Old Faith. The ancient goddesses who preside over rain and fertility are honored and invoked with prayers and offerings.

MAY 6

On this day in the year 1938, the Long Island Church of Aphrodite was established in West Hempstead, New York, by the Reverend Gleb Botkin, a Russian author and son of the court physician to the last Czar of Russia.

MAY 7

On this date (approximately), a festival called the *Thargelia* was celebrated by the ancient Greeks and Ionians in honor of Apollo, the god of the sun, prophecy, music, medicine, and poetry. The festival was held once a year on the sacred island of Delos, the traditional birthplace of Apollo as well as the goddess Artemis.

MAY 8

In Cornwall, England, the annual Furry Dance is performed in the streets of Helston on this day in honor of the old Celtic Horned God in the guise of Robin Hood. The festival, which features street dancing and a daylong procession throughout the town for good fortune, is one of the oldest surviving Springtime ceremonies in the world.

Theosophists commemorate the death of Madame Helena Petrovna Blavatsky on this day, which they call White Lotus Day.

MAY 9

An annual rite called the *Lemuria* was performed on this date in ancient Roman times to appease the restless spirits of the dead (*lemures*), who materialized on this day to haunt the homes where they had once lived. The *Lemuria* was also held on the eleventh and thirteenth of May. As part of the rite, black beans (symbolic of the Underworld) were tossed as offerings to the ghosts and a powerful prayer was recited nine times.

MAY 10

The sacred marriage of the god Shiva to the goddess Meenakshi is celebrated annually on this date by faithful followers in Madurai, India. Sacred hymns are sung and offerings of incense and white flower petals are made at all temples dedicated to Shiva.

Tin Hau, the Chinese goddess of the North Star, is honored annually on this day with a festival in Hong Kong.

MAY 11

On this date in the year 1659, the Puritans of the Massachusetts Bay Colony banned all celebrations of Christmas in the New World after declaring the event to be al Pagan festival of superstition and "a great dishonnor [*sic*] of God."

In England, Christmas festivities had been banned by the Puritans seven years earlier. It wasn't until the year 1660 when Charles II was restored to the throne that the law banning the celebration of Christmas was repealed.

MAY 12

On this date, the annual Cat Parade is celebrated in Belgium in honor of the furry feline, an animal sacred to the ancient Egyptians and often used as a familiar of Witches.

Aranya Sashti, a god of the woodlands, is honored in India on this day with an annual festival. He is identified with the Pagan horned deities Pan and Cernunnos.

MAY 13

On this date in the year 1917, the Goddess in the guise of the Virgin Mary appeared to three peasant children in Fatima, Portugal. The event, which was the first of six divine appearances from May 13 to October 13, drew worldwide attention.

MAY 14

The Festival of the Midnight Sun is celebrated annually on this date by Pagans in far northern Norway. The festival, which pays homage to the ancient Norse goddess of the sun, begins at sunrise and marks the beginning of ten consecutive weeks without the darkness of night.

MAY 15

On this date in ancient times, the Romans performed an annual purification rite consisting of the "sacrifice" of twenty-seven straw puppets to the river god of the Tiber.

MAY 16

On this date in the year 1918, famous Italian spiritualist-medium Eusapia Palladino passed away. She was best remembered for her ability to enter a state of trance and levitate during seances.

MAY 17

In the Philippines, a Neo-Pagan fertility ritual is celebrated every year on this date by married couples who wish to have children. The rites (dedicated to Santa Clara) continue until the nineteenth of May.

MAY 18

The Feast of Twins. On this day, festivals honoring twins are held annually in the African republic of Nigeria. It is widely believed among the Yoruba people that all twins are born with abundant magickal and supernatural powers.

MAY 19

On this day in the year 1780, a strange and unexplained darkness draped most of New England, turning daytime into night.

Many folks believed that a Salem Witch's curse was responsible for the day of darkness, since no other explanation for the phenomenon has ever been found.

MAY 20

On this date, a sacred festival called the *Plynteria* was celebrated annually in ancient Greece. The festival was held in honor of Athena, the goddess of wisdom and battle, and the patroness of the city of Athens (which was named after her), and included the ritual sea cleansing of her statue, followed by prayers in the Parthenon and feasting.

MAY 21

On this date in the year 1911, Peter Hurkos was born in the Netherlands. He developed astonishing psychic powers after recovering from a coma, and became world-famous for solving crimes through the divinatory art of psychometry. He passed away in Los Angeles on May 25, 1988.

On this date in the year 1946, Gwydion Pendderwen was born in Berkeley, California. He was a Celtic bard, a co-founder of the Faery Tradition of Witchcraft, and the founder of a Neo-Pagan networking organization called Nemeton. He died in the Autumn of 1982 as a result of a tragic automobile accident.

MAY 22

On this date (approximately), the Sun enters the astrological sign of Gemini. Persons born under the sign of the Twins are said to be communicative, curious, charming, and often nervous and fickle. Gemini is an air sign and is ruled by the planet Mercury.

Gemini

MAY 23

The *Rosalia,* a sacred rose festival dedicated to the springtime flower-goddess Flora and the love-goddess Venus, was celebrated annually on this date in ancient Rome.

MAY 24

On this day, an annual harvest ritual called Sacred Furrow Day was held in Cambodia. As part of the rite, the farmland would be plowed by members of the royal family in order to appease the ancient gods of the harvest and to ensure the fertility of the land.

The birth of the Greek moon-goddess Artemis (who also presides over hunting and wild beasts) has been celebrated each year on this day since ancient times. As a lunar goddess, she has been an influential archetype for many Witches and worshipers of the contemporary Goddess religion. Artemis is equivalent to the Roman moon-goddess Diana and is identified with Luna, Hecate, and Selene.

MAY 25

In Europe (especially France), this day is sacred to Saint Sarah of the Gypsies and also to an ancient Triple Goddess who rose from the waters of the ocean.

Flora

In ancient Greece, the birthday of Apollo, the twin brother of the goddess Artemis, was celebrated annually on this date.

On this date in the year 1581, famed occultist and alchemist John Dee first realized his natural gift for looking into the future through the art of crystal-gazing. He served for years as the royal astrologer of Queen Elizabeth and had a reputation as a powerful wizard.

MAY 26

Sacred Well Day. On this day, it is traditional for Pagans and Witches (especially in Ireland and Great Britain) to decorate sacred wells with wreaths and to toss offerings of flowers into the water in honor of the deities and spirits of the well. This custom dates back to the ancient Romans, who celebrated an annual well festival called the *Fortinalia*, which took place on this day.

MAY 27

On this day, the Secular Centennial Games were observed in ancient Rome. The goddesses Diana, Prosperina, and the Three Fates were honored in nighttime healing ceremonies.

On this date in the year 1948, Morning Glory Zell was born in Long Beach, California. She is a priestess and vice-president of the Church of All Worlds, and is a practitioner of Celtic Pagan Shamanism.

MAY 28

A sacred rite called the Pythian Games was enacted every four years on this date in ancient Greece. The rite honored the slain serpent-goddess Python, and was celebrated in Delphi, the most venerated shrine in all of Greece.

MAY 29

On this day in ancient times, the god Mars was honored by the farmers of Rome with feasts, prayers, animal sacrifices, and annual rites of purification. The *Ambarvalia* festival was also celebrated on this day in honor of Ceres, Juno, the Lares, and the Family Goddesses.

MAY 30

On this date in the year 1431, French heroine and military leader Joan of Arc was burned alive at the stake as punishment for committing the crimes of Witchcraft, heresy, and "being given to the forbidden arts of magick and divination."

MAY 31

On this day, the annual Triple Blessing of the God Buddha is observed by Theravada Buddhists. To celebrate the god's birth,

(US Library of Congress)

Joan of Arc

enlightenment, and passage into nirvana, shrines and houses are decorated with flowers and special prayer flags. Offerings of flowers, incense, and rice are also made. The Triple Blessing often lasts for three consecutive days.

JUNE

JUNE, the sixth month of the current Gregorian calendar and the first month of Summer, derives its name from the ancient Roman goddess Juno.

The traditional birthstone amulets of June are alexandrite, moonstone, and pearl; and the rose is the month's traditional flower.

June is shared by the astrological signs of Gemini the Twins and Cancer the Crab, and is sacred to the following Pagan deities: Juno, and all gods and goddesses who preside over love, passion, and beauty.

During the month of June, the Great Solar Wheel of the Year is turned to the Summer Solstice, one of the four Lesser Sabbats celebrated each year by Wiccans and modern Witches throughout the world.

JUNE 1

Festival of the Oak Nymph. This Pagan celebration honors all hamadryads (female nature spirits who are believed to inhabit oak trees). Decorate a Pagan altar with acorns and wear some oak leaves in your hair. Kiss an oak tree or place a small offering of some kind before it, and the tree nymphs who dwell within it will surely bestow a blessing upon you.

JUNE 2

Shapatu of Ishtar. A Pagan festival dedicated to the goddess Ishtar is celebrated every year on this date. She is the ancient Assyrian and Babylonian deity who presides over love and fertility as well as war. The birth of the god Apollo is also celebrated on this date.

JUNE 3

The Festival of Cataclysmos is celebrated annually on this date on the Mediterranean island of Cyprus. The seaside ritual consists of prayers for the souls of the departed, traditional water games, and a sacred dance.

In Japan, a Buddhist ritual for young girls is performed annually on this date and is dedicated to the goddesses Befana, Bona Dea, Kuan Yin, Rumina, and Surabhi.

JUNE 4

Whitsunday, an annual Christian festival marking the descent of the Holy Ghost upon the disciples, is celebrated on the seventh Sunday after Easter (which normally falls on or near this date). However, like most Christian holidays, Whitsunday was at one time a Pagan fertility festival. It was celebrated in Europe with a "heathen feast" that marked the death of the spirit of Winter and the birth of the spirit of Summer.

According to English folklore, if a baby comes into the world on Whitsunday, he or she is destined to either commit an act of murder or to be murdered.

JUNE 5

On this date in the year 8498 b.c., the legendary island-continent of Atlantis sank beneath the waves of the Atlantic Ocean in a cataclysm believed to have been brought on by the anger of the great god Zeus.

To ensure an abundant harvest, a sacred Corn Dance is held each year at this time at San Ildefonso Pueblo in the southwestern United States. It is dedicated to the Earth Mothers and the nature spirits known as the Rain People.

JUNE 6

On this date (approximately), an annual festival to honor ancestral spirits begins in Nigeria. The festival, which lasts for one week, consists of street dancing, offerings of food and gifts to the Egungun, and ecstatic trance.

In Thrace, an ancient country in the southeastern part of the Balkan Peninsula, a festival called the *Bendidia* was held each year on this date. It was dedicated to the lunar goddess Bendi.

JUNE 7

The *Vestalia*, an annual festival in honor of the hearth-goddess Vesta, began on this date in ancient Rome. During the eight-day-long festival, the shrine of Vesta was opened to married women. After the festival was over, the shrine was once again forbidden to all except the goddess' attendant vestal virgins.

JUNE 8

In many Japanese villages, an ancient rice festival is held annually on this date. Women wearing traditional kimonos recite prayers and light rice-straw fires to honor the god of the rice and to bless the crops.

In China, the Grain in Ear festival is celebrated at this time. The grain gods are honored with old rituals to ensure a harvest of plenty.

JUNE 9

On this date in 1892, Grace Cook (a popular spiritualist medium and founder of the White Eagle Lodge) was born in London, England. Her first psychic vision of Indian Chief White Eagle and other Native American spirits occurred early in her childhood. With the aid of her spirit guide, she authored many books on healing and spiritual growth. She believed that after her death (which occurred on September 3, 1979), her spirit would be reincarnated in Egypt.

JUNE 10

On this date in the year 1692, a woman named Bridget Bishop was hanged on Gallows Hill in Salem, Massachusetts, after being found guilty of the crime of Witchcraft. She was the first person to be publicly executed in the infamous Salem Witch Trials.

JUNE 11

On this date in 1912, spiritualist-medium Ruth Montgomery was born in Princeton, Indiana. Her interest in the world of the occult began in 1956, when she first began attending seances. She has written numerous bestselling occult books and is famous for her gift of communicating with spirit guides through automatic writing.

JUNE 12

Light gold-colored candles on your altar and wear oak leaves in your hair to honor the Greek god Zeus, who is traditionally honored on this day.

In Korea, rice farmers wash their hair in a stream on this day as part of an annual ritual to dispel bad luck and to ensure an abundant crop. This ritual has taken place since ancient times.

JUNE 13

On this date in the year 1884, Gerald Gardner was born in Lancashire, England. Nicknamed King of the Witches, he went on to become a famous and well-respected Wiccan author and the founder of the Gardnerian tradition of the modern Wicca religion. He died on February 12, 1964.

Irish poet and ceremonial magician William Butler Yeats was also born on this date in the year 1865.

JUNE 14

In ancient Rome, the goddess Minerva (patroness of wisdom and the arts, and a deity of battle) was honored annually on this date at her sacred festival, the Lesser Quinquatrus of Minerva.

In India, this is a day sacred to Jagannath, a benevolent incarnation of the god Vishnu. An annual festival in honor of him is celebrated in the city of Puri on the East Coast of India.

JUNE 15

On this date in the year 1648, Margaret Jones of Charlestown, Massachusetts, was executed in Boston for practicing Witchcraft and magickal healing. This was the first pre-Salem Witch execution to be officially recorded in the Commonwealth of Massachusetts.

JUNE 16

Silver Chalice Day. Every year on this date, Wiccan friends and coven members gather together in a circle to rejoice and share a traditional silver chalice of wine (or fruit juice) consecrated in the names of the Goddess and Her consort, the Horned God. Many Pagan handfastings and Wiccanings are performed by coven priestesses around this time of the month.

On this date in the year 1881, famous Voodoo Queen Marie Laveau died in her home in New Orleans, Louisiana.

JUNE 17

An annual purification ritual to drive away the evil spirits of the rainy season takes place on this date in Nara, Japan. Lily stalks are blessed by seven white-robed priestesses, and a traditional dance is performed.

Also on this date, Eurydice (a tree nymph who was transformed into an Underworld goddess after dying from a serpent bite) was honored annually in ancient Greece.

JUNE 18

The annual Dragon Boat Festival (which at one time was a Pagan summer solstice ritual to appease the dragon gods of the rivers) is celebrated on this date in China in honor of the martyred poet, Qu Yuan.

In ancient Rome, the goddess Anna was honored on this day with an annual religious festival.

JUNE 19

The Feast of the Holy Ghost, a weeklong religious festival, begins annually on this date in Brazil.

In ancient Rome, the Day of All Heras was celebrated annually on this date in honor of the Goddess within as well as all wisewomen.

JUNE 20

On this day, Pagans in parts of England celebrate the Day of Cerridwen in honor of the ancient Celtic goddess of fertility. Vervain (the herb most sacred to Cerridwen) is burned in small cauldron pots as an offering to the goddess, green ribbons are tied to trees, and green candles are lit on altars dedicated to her.

JUNE 21

On the first day of Summer (which normally occurs on or near this date), the Summer Solstice Sabbat is celebrated by Wiccans and Witches throughout the world. Summer Solstice (which is also known as Midsummer, Alban Hefin, and Litha) marks the longest day of the year when the Sun is at its zenith. In certain Wiccan traditions, the Summer Solstice symbolizes the end of the reign of the waxing year's Oak-King, who is now replaced by his successor, the Holly-King of the waning year. (The Holly-King will rule until the Winter Solstice.) It is the ideal time for divinations, healing rituals, and the cutting of divining rods and wands.

On Midsummer Day, the people of ancient Russia worshiped the fertility goddess Kupala. To ensure female fertility and abundant crops, she was honored with bonfires, sacrifices of cockarels, and special wreaths that were cast into the rivers.

JUNE 22

On this date (approximately), the Sun enters the astrological sign of Cancer. Persons born under the sign of the Crab are said to be family and home-oriented, nurturing, sympathetic, and often very moody. Cancer is a water sign and is ruled by the Moon.

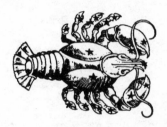

Cancer

JUNE 23

In parts of Ireland and Great Britain, Pagans celebrate an annual festival on this date called the Day of Cu Chulainn. It is dedicated to the legendary Irish folk hero of the same name and to the ancient Pagan fertility god known as the Green Man.

Saint John's Eve. This night is a traditional time for Witches to gather herbs for spells and love potions, for it is believed that the magickal properties of plants are at their peak on this mystical night.

JUNE 24

On this date, an ancient Egyptian festival known as The Burning of the Lamps is celebrated in Sais, a city on the Nile delta.

In pre-Christian times, the festival of *Fors Fortuna* was

celebrated annually on this date in the city of Rome to honor and receive favorable blessings from the goddess Fortuna.

A sun-god festival called *Inti Raymi* was celebrated annually on this date by the ancient Incas of Peru. Llamas were ritually slaughtered and their entrails were used by priests for divining the future.

On this date in the year 1950, Reformed Alexandrian Witch and author Janet Farrar was born in London, England.

JUNE 25

Gay Wiccan Pride Day. This is a time for gay and lesbian Wiccans from around the world to unite and celebrate life, love, and the Goddess. Come out of the proverbial "broom closet" and be proud of who you are!

A centuries-old women's festival is held in India every year on this date in honor of the goddess Parvati.

JUNE 26

According to ancient Icelandic legend, every year at noon on this date, the tip of the shadow of Mount Scartaris points to the secret entrance of "Centre Earth," in which dwell giant humanlike creatures and prehistoric monsters.

Salavi, the Spruce Tree Rain God, is honored annually on this day by a Native American corn-ripening ceremony. This day is also sacred to the Corn Mothers and the Kachinis.

JUNE 27

A centuries-old Native American Sun Dance ritual is performed annually on this date by many Plains Indian tribes in honor of the Summer Sun. As part of the ceremony, a sacred crow totem is decorated with black feathers.

On this date in the year 1956, prolific Wiccan author Scott Cunningham was born in Royal Oak, Michigan.

JUNE 28

Every year on this day, the birth of Hemera (the ancient Greek goddess of day) is celebrated. Festivals in her honor begin at sunrise and last until the setting of the sun.

On this date in the year 1916, Reformed Alexandrian Witch and author Stewart Farrar was born in Highams Park, Essex, England.

JUNE 29

On this date in Appleton, England, the boughs of a large and very old hawthorn tree are decorated with flowers, flags, and ribbons as part of a centuries-old Pagan tree-worship ritual known as Bawming the Thorn.

This is a sacred day to Papa Legba, a powerful loa in the Voodoo religion. Originally a Dahomean sun god, Papa Legba is worshiped as the spirit-master of pathways and crossroads, and is the most important deity of the Vodoun pantheon.

JUNE 30

Day of Aestas. The ancient Roman corn-goddess of Summer is honored each year on this sacred day. Corn bread is traditionally served at Wiccan gatherings.

This day is sacred to the Pagan and Native American goddesses Ceres, Changing Woman, Chicomecoatl, the Corn Mothers, Demeter, Gaia, Ge, Hestia, Iatiku, Oraea, Pachamama, Spider Woman, and Tonantzin.

JULY

JULY, the seventh month of the current Gregorian calendar and the second month of Summer's rule, derives its name from *Julius* (Julius Caesar).

The traditional birthstone amulet of July is the ruby; and the larkspur and the water lily are the month's traditional flowers.

July is shared by the astrological signs of Cancer the Crab and Leo the Lion, and is sacred to the following Pagan deities: Apt (or Apet), Athena, Sothis, Spider Woman, and Rosea.

JULY 1

The month of July opens in Nepal with the *Naga Panchami* festival, which is devoted to the Snake-Gods called Nagas. Sacred snake images are displayed on religious altars, offerings are made at snake holes, and parades featuring live serpents fill the main streets of many villages.

In Japan, this day is sacred to Fuji, the ancient Japanese goddess of fire. Fuji is also regarded as the grandmother of Japan, and on this special day (which also marks the start of Mount Fuji Climbing Season) she is honored with prayers and burnt offerings.

JULY 2

On this day in ancient times, the citizens of Rome celebrated the Feast of Expectant Mothers. At temples throughout the city, all pregnant women gathered to receive blessings and honor Bona Dea, Carmenta, Lucina, and other goddesses associated with birth and fertility.

JULY 3

The New Year of the Seminole Indian tribe of Florida begins on this date, and is celebrated with an annual Green Corn Dance honoring the new corn crop.

In Italy, this day is sacred to the Witch of Gaeta; in Greece, the goddess Athena is honored.

JULY 4

U.S. Independence Day. On this day, the anniversary of the adoption of the Declaration of Independence in 1776, the official "birth" of the United States is celebrated by Pagans and non-Pagans alike. On this day, many patriotic American wiccans honor and give thanks to Lady Liberty, and perform magickal spells and rituals for the benefit of the country.

Day of Pax. On this day in ancient times, Pax (a Roman goddess of peace and harmony, identified with the Greek goddess Concordia) was honored with feasting and revelry.

Also on this day, the spirits of the mountains are honored by the Mescalero Apache Gahan Ceremonial, while the Great God who dwells within the fire of the Sun is paid homage to by the Ute Indian tribe of Utah and Colorado, who perform an annual Sun Dance.

JULY 5

Every year on this date, the Aphelion of the Earth takes place. When this occurs, the planet Earth reaches the point in its orbit when it is farthest from the Sun. Many astrologers consider this to be a highly significant event.

In ancient Egypt, this day was held sacred to Maat, the goddess who presides over truth and wisdom.

JULY 6

This is a day sacred to all horned goddesses of the ancient Pagan religions: the Deer Mothers, Europa, Hathor, Hera, Io, Ishtar, Isis, Juno, Luna, Nephthys, Pasiphae, Selene, and so forth.

In Spain, the annual Running of the Bulls takes place on this day. The bull symbolizes fertility and the male procreative power, and is a sacred animal to Apis, Baal, Bacchus, Dionysos Zagreus, Dumuzi, Enki, Freya, Menwer, the Minotaur, Moloch, Sin, Thor, and Yama.

JULY 7

In Japan, the *Tanabata* (Star Festival) takes place annually on this day and celebrates the reunion of the two celestial lovers who bridged a raging river with their own bodies.

In China, the annual Feast of the Milky Way (*Chih Nu*) takes place each year on this day to celebrate the romantic encounter between Vega the Weaver Maid and Aquila the Herd Boy.

JULY 8

On this date in ancient Rome, a nature festival known as the *Nonae Caprotinae* (Nones of the Wild Figs) was celebrated in honor of the goddess Juno, the Great Mother. It is believed to be one of the oldest of the women's festivals.

In Tomar, Portugal, there is an annual parade in which girls balance flower-covered pillars of bread on their heads. This parade is believed to ward off the spirits of illness for the remainder of the year.

JULY 9

In ancient Greece, a six-day festival called the *Panathenaea* began on this day every four years. It was held in honor of the goddess Athena.

On this day, Pagans around the world celebrate the divine birthdays of the wine- and fertility-god Dionysus and the Greek goddess Rhea.

On this date in the year 1992, Herman Slater (Wiccan High Priest, well-known occult author, and proprietor of The Magickal Childe bookstore and Witchcraft supply shop in New York City) lost his battle against AIDS. His death was a great loss to the magickal community.

JULY 10

Day of Holda. On this day, the Anglo-Saxon and Norse goddess of the Underworld is honored annually with prayers, the lighting of black candles, and offerings of rose petals.

On this day (approximately) a centuries-old festival is held in Douai, France. Wickerwork giants are paraded through the streets of the city to drive away evil-natured spirits and demons.

JULY 11

In ancient times, the Greek deities Kronos (Father Time) and Rhea (Mother Earth) were honored with an annual religious festival called the *Kronia*, which took place on this date in the city of Athens.

JULY 12

According to an age-old superstition, a child who comes into the world on the twelfth day of July ("the luckiest day of the year") will be destined for a life of wealth and great success.

Yama, the Buddhist god of death and the Underworld, is honored annually on this day in Tibet with an ancient festival known as the Old Dances.

This day is also sacred to the goddess Dikaiosune, an ancient deity who presides over justice.

JULY 13

On this day, the birth of the vegetation- and fertility-god Osiris is celebrated by many Wiccans of the Egyptian tradition. The annual death and rebirth of Osiris personifies the self-renewing vitality and fertility of nature.

John Dee

In the country of Japan, the annual *Bon* festival is celebrated on this date in honor of ancestral spirits.

On this date in the year 1527, John Dee was born in London, England. He was renowned as an alchemist and was skilled in the arts of wizardry. For many years he served as the royal astrologer of Queen Elizabeth I. He died in poverty in the year 1608.

JULY 14

On this day, the birth of the Egyptian falcon-headed god Horus is celebrated by many Wiccans of the Egyptian tradition. Light a royal-blue altar candle and burn some frankincense and myrrh as a fragrant offering to him.

On this date in the year 1988, a series of mysterious crop circles began to appear in a wheat field near Silbury Hill in southwestern England.

JULY 15

On this day, the birth of the Egyptian god Set (or Seth) is celebrated by many Wiccans of the Egyptian tradition. Set is an ancient god of darkness and the magickal arts.

In China, this day is sacred to Ti-Tsang, the ruler of the dark Underworld. He is honored with an annual Festival of the Dead.

JULY 16

On this day, thousands of Haitians begin an annual pilgrimage to the Saut d' Eau waterfall, which is sacred to Erzulie Freda (the Voodoo loa of love and beauty) and is believed to possess miraculous healing powers.

JULY 17

On this date in the year 1992, a Pagan-based radio show called *The Witching Hour* (hosted by Winter Wren and Don Lewis) made its debut on radio station WONX in Evanston, Illinois (a suburb of Chicago).

In China, the sun-goddess Amaterasu is honored annually on this day with a Shinto procession called the *Amaterasu-Omikami*.

JULY 18

On this date, the birthday of Lu Pan (the patron saint of Chinese carpenters and house builders) is celebrated annually by workmen (and women) throughout the city of Hong Kong.

On this day, the birth of Nepthys (the Egyptian goddess of death, and sister of Isis) is celebrated.

This day is also sacred to the goddesses Arstat and Copper Woman.

JULY 19

On this day, the birth of the Egyptian goddess Isis is celebrated by many Wiccans of the Egyptian tradition. Isis is an ancient Mother-goddess of fertility and a Neo-Pagan deity associated with magick and enchantment.

On this date in the year 1692, Rebecca Nurse, Sarah Good, and Susanna Martin were hanged on Salem's Gallows Hill as punishment for the crime of Witchcraft.

JULY 20

On this date in the year 1980, famous Dutch clairvoyant Gerard Croiset passed away. He was renowned as both a psychic healer and psychic criminologist.

In Lithuania, the ancient goddesses of love are invoked during an annual lover's festival called The Binding of the Wreaths, which takes place on this day.

JULY 21

The Mayan New Year is celebrated annually on this date in South America. This is a very sacred day to the Maya, who welcome their New Year with feasts and prayers in honor of the old gods.

JULY 22

On this date in the year 1930, the first sighting of the famous monster of Loch Ness was officially recorded in Scotland. Old Nessie (as the monster has been affectionately nicknamed) has since been witnessed by thousands of people and continues to attract countless numbers of tourists with cameras to Loch Ness each year.

JULY 23

The festival of *Neptunalia* was celebrated annually on this date in ancient Rome to honor Neptune, the lord of the sea. In Italy, many modern Witches honor Neptune on this day by lighting a blue candle, inscribed with his trident symbol and anointed with seawater, and placing it on an altar along with various objects from the sea (such as seashells, pieces of drift-wood, and so forth).

JULY 24

On this date (approximately) the Sun enters the astrological sign of Leo. Persons born under the sign of the Lion are said to be generous, romantic, proud, and often egotistical. Leo is a fire sign and is ruled by the Sun.

Leo

JULY 25

In Osaka, Japan, a thousand-year-old festival of paper dolls is celebrated annually on this date. The handmade dolls are traditionally rubbed on the bodies of the faithful to absorb illnesses, negativity, and evil spirits. The dolls are then taken to a bridge and dropped into the waters of the river below.

JULY 26

The *Kachina* ceremony is celebrated annually on this date by the Native American tribe of the Hopi in Arizona. The kachinas (ancient spirits that are believed to guide and protect the Hopi people) are honored with religious ceremonies and a cycle of dances.

JULY 27

Day of Hatshepsut. On this day each year, the eighteenth dynasty Healer Queen of ancient Egypt is honored. Healing rituals are performed by many Wiccans, especially those of the Egyptian traditions.

In Belgium, a centuries-old event known as The Procession of Witches takes place every year on this day.

JULY 28

In the olden days of Pagan Europe, the great thunder-god Thor was honored on this date with prayers for protection of the crops against destructive storms.

JULY 29

On this day in Tarascon, France, the annual festival of *Tarasque* takes place. The festival, celebrated since Pagan times, commemorates the capture of a mythical fire-breathing dragon. A decorated dragon float is paraded through the streets of the city and touched by spectators for good luck and to ward off evil.

JULY 30

In Nova Scotia, this day is sacred to the Micmac Indian tribe. It is believed that all those who are wed or christened at this time will be blessed with happiness and good health by the Great Spirits. Saint Ann (the Mother Goddess) and Gloosca (the Father God) are honored.

JULY 31
August Eve, Lammas Eve,
the Eve of Lughnasadh

In pre-Christian times, the *Oidhche Lugnasa* was celebrated by the Celts on this night in honor of their solar deity named Lugh. His annual sacrifice at the end of the harvest ensured the fertility of the corn and grain for the next growing season.

An old August Eve tradition in rural Scotland is predicting the following year's marriages and deaths by throwing sickles into the air and then drawing omens from the position in which they fall.

On this date in the year 1831, famous mystic and spiritualist-medium Madame Helena Petrovna Blavatsky was born in the Ukraine.

AUGUST

AUGUST, the eighth month of the current Gregorian calendar and the third month of Summer's rule, derives its name from *Augustus* (Augustus Caesar).

The traditional birthstone amulets of August are the peridot and the sardonyx; and the gladiolus and the poppy are the month's traditional flowers.

August is shared by the astrological signs of Leo the Lion and Virgo the Virgin, and is sacred to the following Pagan deities: Ceres, the Corn Mother, Demeter, John Barleycorn, Lugh, and all goddesses who preside over agriculture.

During the month of August, the Great Solar Wheel of the Year is turned to Lammas, one of the four Grand Sabbats celebrated each year by Wiccans and modern Witches throughout the world.

AUGUST 1

On this day, the Lammas Sabbat is celebrated by Wiccans and Witches throughout the world. Lammas (which is also known as Lughnasadh, August Eve, and the First Festival of Harvest) marks the start of the harvest season and is a time when the fertility aspect of the sacred union of the Goddess and Horned God is honored. The making of corn dollies (small figures fashioned from braided straw) is a centuries-old Pagan custom which is carried on by many modern Witches as part of the Lammas Sabbat rite. The corn dollies are placed on the Sabbat altar to represent the Mother Goddess who presides over the harvest. It is customary on each Lammas to make or buy a new corn dolly and then burn the old one from the past year for good luck.

On this day in the country of Macedonia, Neo-Pagans celebrate the Day of the Dryads, an annual nature festival dedicated to the maiden spirits who inhabit and rule over forests and trees.

AUGUST 2

On this day, the Feast of Anahita is celebrated in honor of the ancient Persian goddess Anahita, a deity associated with love and lunar powers.

Lady Godiva Day is celebrated annually on this date in the village of Coventry, England, with a medieval-style parade led by a nude woman on horseback.

AUGUST 3

The harvest season begins on this date in Japan with an annual festival called the *Aomori Nebuta*. Bamboo effigies with grotesquely painted faces are paraded through the streets in order to drive away the spirits of sleep.

AUGUST 4

Each year on this date, it was believed that the waters of Scotland's Loch-mo-Naire became charged with miraculous magickal powers to heal all who drank it or bathed in it. For many years it was a custom for those who visited Loch-mo-Naire to toss in a coin of silver as an offering to the benevolent spirits that dwelled within the lake.

AUGUST 5

Many folks still believe in this ancient superstition: if you make a secret wish while looking up at the new moon (which normally begins on or near this date in August), your wish will be granted before the year is through.

AUGUST 6

On this date in the year 1817, a huge creature described as a sea-serpent was spotted in the ocean near Gloucester harbor in Massachusetts. Coincidentally, on this same date in the year 1948, a similar creature was seen by the crew of the British naval frigate *Daedalus*.

This day is sacred to the Cherokee Earth-Goddess Elihino and her sister Igaehindvo, the sacred goddess of the Sun.

AUGUST 7

In ancient Egypt, the cow-headed goddess Hathor was honored on this day by an annual festival known as Breaking the Nile. The festival, which was also dedicated to all water and river goddesses, celebrated the rising of the fertile waters of the mystical River Nile.

In ancient Greece, the annual mourning ceremony called

the *Adonia* was held on this date in honor of the dying hero-god Adonis.

AUGUST 8

According to the Christian Church calendar, the Virgin Mary was born on this day.

The Eve of the Festival of Venus was celebrated annually on this date by the ancient Romans. On this night, the goddess of love and beauty was honored and invoked with prayers, love songs, libations, and passionate lovemaking. It

Venus
Detail from Botticelli's Birth of Venus

was also a time when sorceresses performed all forms of love magick and marriage-mate divinations.

AUGUST 9

On this date, many Wiccans from around the world celebrate the annual Feast of the Fire Spirits. Dried mandrake root or yarrow herb is cast into fires as offerings to the Salamanders.

AUGUST 10

A centuries-old festival called Ghanta Karna Day is celebrated annually around this time of August in the Himalayan kingdom of Nepal. The event celebrates the death of Ghanta Karna, a blood-thirsty Hindu demon who haunts crossroads and is the sworn enemy of the god Vishnu.

AUGUST 11

On this day, an Irish fertility festival known as the Puck Fair begins. The medieval-style festival, which pays homage to the mischievous sprite Robin Goodfellow, continues for three consecutive days.

Oddudua, the "Mother of All Gods," is honored on this day by followers of the Santeria religion in Africa and South America.

AUGUST 12

The goddess Isis and her search for Osiris (her brother and consort) is commemorated on this day by the *Lychnapsia* (Festival of the Lights of Isis.) Dried rose petals and vervain are burned in small cauldron pots or incense burners as offerings to Isis, and green candles are lit in her honor.

AUGUST 13

On this date, the major Pagan festival of Hecate is traditionally held at moonrise. Hecate, the mysterious goddess of darkness and protectress of all Witches, is a personification of the Moon and the dark side of the female principle.

AUGUST 14

Every year on this date, a "burryman" (a man wearing a costume of thistle burrs, and representing an ancient fertility god) walks through the streets in many of the fishing villages along the coast of Scotland, collecting donations from the villagers. The origin of the burryman remains a mystery.

AUGUST 15

Festival of Vesta. The ancient Roman goddess of the hearth was honored annually on this date in ancient times. Many modern Witches light six red candles and cast herbs into hearth-fires on this day to honor Vesta and to receive her blessings for family and home.

AUGUST 16

Salem Heritage Day in Massachusetts

On this date in the year 1987, the first Harmonic Con-ver-gence was observed worldwide during the Grand Trine (the alignment of all nine planets in our solar system). The event, which lasted for two consecutive days, was believed to be the beginning of five years of peace and spiritual purification. Thousands of New Age enthusiasts gathered at various sacred sites to dance, chant, meditate, and tune into the positive energies of the Earth and the universe.

AUGUST 17

Festival of Diana. Every year on this date, the goddess of chastity, hunting, and the moon was honored by the ancient Romans.

This a special day of feasting, mirth, and magick-making for many Dianic Wiccans, since Diana is the most sacred goddess of their tradition.

On this date in the year 1950, Oglala Sioux mystic and medicine man Nicholas Black Elk died in Manderson, South Dakota. He was known for his great powers of prophecy and healing, and was an adherent of the Ghost Dance, a short-lived Native American religious movement which ended in a tragic massacre at Wounded Knee, South Dakota, in 1890.

Diana

AUGUST 18

On this date, the annual Festival of Hungry Ghosts is celebrated throughout China with burnt offerings to the spirits of the dead.

On this date in the year 1634, a parish priest named Father Urbain Grandier was found guilty of bewitching a group of nuns at a convent in Loudun, France, and causing them to be possessed by demons. He was condemned to be tortured and then burned alive in the public square of Saint Croix.

(Mary Evans Picture Library, London)

Father Urbain Grandier

AUGUST 19

In ancient Rome, a wine-harvest celebration known as the *Vinalia Rustica* was held each year on this date. It was dedicated to the goddess Venus of the Grape Vine and also to Minerva.

On this date in the year 1692, the Reverend George Burroughs and John Willard were put to death on Salem's infamous Gallows Hill as punishment for the crime of Witchcraft.

AUGUST 20

On this date in the year 1612, ten women and men known as the Lancashire Witches were executed on the gallows in one of England's most famous Witch trials of the seventeenth century. Ironically, the nine-year-old girl who had supplied the court with incriminating evidence against the Witches was herself found guilty of Witchcraft twenty-two years later and executed in the second great Witch trial of Lancashire.

AUGUST 21

The *Consualia*, a harvest festival celebrating the storing of the new crop, was held annually on this date by the ancient Romans. Also celebrated on this date was the muscular deity Hercules, who was honored with a sacrifice at one of his shrines in the city of Rome. His annual festival was called the *Heraclia*.

AUGUST 22

On this date in the year 1623, the Order of the Rosy Cross (a secret sect associated with alchemy and reincarnation) was established in Paris, France. The mysterious Rosicrucian brotherhood was condemned by officials of the Church as worshipers of Satan.

This day is sacred to Nu Kwa, an ancient Chinese goddess identified with the healing goddess Kuan Yin.

AUGUST 23

The *Volcanalia* festival was celebrated annually on this date in ancient Rome. It was dedicated to Vulcan, the god of volcanic eruptions, and celebrated by frying fish alive to ward off accidental fires.

Each year on this date in Athens, the ancient Greeks celebrated a festival dedicated to Nemesis, the goddess who presided over the fate of all men and women.

Virgo

AUGUST 24

On this date (approximately), the Sun enters the astrological sign of Virgo. Persons born under the sign of the Virgin are said to be analytical, organized, meticulous, and often prone to being perfectionists. Virgo is an earth sign and is ruled by the planet Mercury.

AUGUST 25

An annual harvest festival called the *Opiconsiva* was celebrated on this date in ancient Rome in honor of the fertility and success goddess Ops (Rhea). Later in the year, she was honored again at the *Opalia* festival on December 19 (the third day of the *Saturnalia*).

AUGUST 26

The periodic rebirth of the Hindu god Krishna (eighth and principal avatar of Vishnu) is celebrated by his faithful worshipers at midnight services on this date.

In the country of Finland, this is the annual Feast Day of Ilmatar (or Luonnotar), known as the Water Mother. According to mythology, she created the Earth out of chaos.

AUGUST 27

Consus, the god of the grain-store, was celebrated annually on this date by the ancient Romans. Sacrifices were made in his honor, and all beasts of burden were embellished with wreaths of flowers and given a day of rest.

The Festival of Krishna is celebrated annually on this day in the country of India. It is also a sacred day dedicated to Devaki, the Mother-Goddess.

AUGUST 28

In the country of Norway, a Pagan festival celebrating the harvest is held on this date each year. Ancient Norse gods and goddesses are invoked to protect the spirit of the harvest throughout the dark half of the year.

AUGUST 29
Ancient Egyptian New Year

On this date in Nigeria, the Yoruba people celebrate the *Gelede*, an annual ritual of dancing and wearing of masks to drive away evil sorceresses.

In pre-Christian times, a festival called the Pardon of the Sea was celebrated annually in Brittany. It was originally dedicated to Ahes, a Pagan goddess of the sea, and was later Christianized into the Feast of Saint Anne.

AUGUST 30

In Bengal, India, gruesome human sacrifices to the Indian earth-goddess Tari Pennu were made annually on this date as late as the mid-nineteenth century. After the sacrifice, a shaman would eat a bit of the victim's flesh, and then the rest of the remains would be dismembered, burned, and scattered over a plowed field to ensure the fertility of future crops.

AUGUST 31

To purify the family spirits, Eyos (masqueraders wearing demon costumes concealed by white robes) walk through the streets of Lagos every year on this date. The Ritual Walk of the Eyos is a religious custom that dates back to ancient times.

On this date in the year 1934, Wiccan author Raymond Buckland was born in London, England. He founded the Seax-Wica tradition of Witchcraft, helped to introduce modern Wicca into the United States, and opened the first American Museum of Witchcraft and Magic.

In India, a women's festival of purification is held each year on this day. It is called the *Anant Chaturdasi*, and is dedicated to the ancient serpent-goddess Ananta, who symbolizes the female life force.

SEPTEMBER

SEPTEMBER, the ninth month of the current Gregorian calendar and the first month of Autumn, derives its name from *septem,* the Latin word meaning "seven," as September was the seventh month of the old Roman calendar.

The traditional birthstone amulet of September is the blue sapphire; and the aster and the morning glory are the month's traditional flowers.

September is shared by the astrological signs of Virgo the Virgin and Libra the Scales (or Balance), and is sacred to the following Pagan deities: Persephone, Thor, and the Wiccan Goddess in Her aspect of the Mother.

During the month of September, the Great Solar Wheel of the Year is turned to the Autumnal Equinox, one of the four Lesser Sabbats celebrated each year by Wiccans and modern Witches throughout the world.

SEPTEMBER 1

On this date in the sixth century *b.c.*, the Persian prophet and mystic known as Zoroaster was born. He founded the religion of Zoroastrianism, which teaches that all of mankind is trapped in a perpetual battle between good spirits and bad spirits.

SEPTEMBER 2

On this date in ancient Athens, an annual Grape Vine Festival was held in honor of the Greek deities Ariadne and Dionysus. In Crete, Ariadne was worshiped as a goddess of the Moon, and Dionysus as the son of Semele (who was also a goddess of the Moon).

SEPTEMBER 3

On this day, the annual Path Clearing Festival (*Akwambo*) is held by the Akan people of Ghana to honor and receive blessings from the ancient god of the sacred well.

The Maidens of the Four Directions are honored on this day each year by a Hopi Indian women's healing ceremony called *Lakon*.

SEPTEMBER 4

At sunrise on this day, the Changing Woman Ceremony is held annually by the Native American tribe of the Apache in Arizona. The rite, which lasts for four consecutive days, marks the coming of age of a pubescent girl, who ritually transforms into the spirit-goddess known as Changing Woman and blesses all who are in attendance.

SEPTEMBER 5

In ancient Rome, the Roman Games, in honor of the god Jupiter, began annually on this date and lasted until the thirteenth day of September.

Ganesh, the elephant-headed Hindu god of good luck and prosperity, is honored on this day throughout India with a parade and a festival of rejoicing.

SEPTEMBER 6

An ancient Inca blood festival called the *Situa* was held annually on this date to ward off the evil spirits of illness and disease. As part of the ceremony, parents would eat a special cake consecrated with the blood of their offspring.

SEPTEMBER 7

Healer's Day. This is a special day dedicated to all women and men who possess the Goddess-given gift of healing and who use it unselfishly to help others.

Daena, the Maiden Goddess of the Parsees, is honored on this date each year with a religious festival in India.

SEPTEMBER 8

On this date in the year 1875, the Theosophical Society (an organization dedicated to spreading occult lore and ancient wisdom) was founded by Madame Helena Petrova Blavatsky, Henry Steel Olcott, William Judge, and other occultists.

SEPTEMBER 9

In China, chrysanthemum wine is traditionally drunk on this day each year to ensure long life and to honor Tao

Yuan-Ming, a Chinese poet who was deified as the god of the chrysanthemum.

SEPTEMBER 10

The Ceremony of the Deermen is held every year at dawn on the first Monday after Wakes Sunday (which normally falls on or near this date). As part of the ceremony, held at Abbots Bromley in Staffordshire, England, the Deerman, wearing antlers and carrying clubs surmounted with deers' heads, escort two young men dressed as Robin Hood and Maid Marian across the village.

On this date in the year 1930, Carl Llewellyn Weschcke (former Wiccan high priest and owner of Llewellyn Publications) was born in Saint Paul, Minnesota. In 1972 he was initiated by Lady Sheba into the American Celtic tradition of Witchcraft, and in 1973 he helped to organize the Council of American Witches.

SEPTEMBER 11

In Egypt, a centuries-old festival called the Day of Queens is celebrated annually on this date in honor of Hatshepsut, Nefertiti, and Cleopatra, who were also regarded as goddesses.

SEPTEMBER 12

On this date in the year 1902, actress Margaret Hamilton was born in Cleveland, Ohio. She is best known for her memorable role as the Wicked Witch of the West in the 1939 film *The Wizard of Oz*. She died on May 16, 1985, in Salisbury, Connecticut.

SEPTEMBER 13

Egyptian All Souls' Day. Every year on this date, the ancient Egyptians celebrated a religious festival known as The

Ceremony of Lighting the Fire. Sacred fires were lit in temples in honor of the spirits of the dead and the goddess Nephthys, protectress of the dead and Queen of the Underworld.

SEPTEMBER 14

In ancient Rome, the Feast of the Holy Cross was celebrated on this date in commemoration of a supernatural vision of a cross in the sky, as well as a battle victory of Roman Emperor Constantine I.

On this date in the year 1692, the Witch trial of two Pilgrim women opened in Stamford, Connecticut. One was found not guilty; the other was convicted and sentenced to die, but was later reprieved by an investigating committee.

(J. Schliebe, Das Kloster, 1846)

Agrippa von Nettesheim

On this date in the year 1486, ceremonial magician Agrippa von Nettesheim was born in Cologne, France. He was skilled in the arts of divination, numerology, and astrology, and wrote several books that had a great influence over Western occultism. He died in Grenoble, France in the year 1535.

SEPTEMBER 15

The full moon of September, known as the Harvest Moon, normally begins on or around this date. Many believe it to possess great magickal powers, and numerous superstitions are connected with it. Harvest Moon rituals are performed throughout the world on the first night of the full moon by many Witches and Pagans, especially those who dwell in the country.

SEPTEMBER 16

Feast of Saint Cornely. On this day, villagers and farmers who live in Brittany honor Saint Cornely, the patron of horned animals who is believed to have created the Carnac megaliths by magickally transforming enemy soldiers into stone. At midnight, oxen are blessed in a shrine dedicated to him.

SEPTEMBER 17

On this date in the year 1964, *Bewitched* (the first television sitcom about a Witch) made its debut on ABC-TV. It became an instant hit and received twenty-two Emmy nominations.

In ancient Greece, the goddess Demeter was honored annually on this date with a festival of secret rites.

SEPTEMBER 18

In the town of Berkshire, England, a centuries-old celebration known as Scouring the White Horse begins on this date. The festival of games and athletic competition takes place on a hillside carved with the huge figure of a galloping steed, and lasts for two consecutive days.

SEPTEMBER 19

On this day in ancient Babylonia, an annual festival of prayers and feasts took place in honor of Gula, the goddess of birth.

On this date in the year 1692, Giles Corey (a Massachusetts man charged with the crime of Witchcraft) was pressed to death by large stones in Salem for refusing to acknowledge the Court's right to try him.

SEPTEMBER 20

The Spring Equinox (South of the Equator) was celebrated approximately on this date by the ancient Incas. It was a time for honoring the Sun God, feasting, rejoicing, animal sacrifices, and divinations. Festivals were also held on this date throughout South America to celebrate the birthday of the god Quetzalcoatl.

SEPTEMBER 21

Saint Matthew's Day. In many parts of the world, this is a traditional day for performing divinations of all kinds. In Germany, fortune-telling wreaths of straw and evergreen, made on this day by young girls, were used for love divination.

In ancient Greece, the birth of the goddess Athena was celebrated annually on this day.

SEPTEMBER 22

On the first day of Autumn (which normally occurs on or near this date), the Autumn Equinox Sabbat is celebrated by

Wiccans and Witches throughout the world. Autumn Equinox (which is also known as the Fall Sabbat, Alban Elfed, and the Second Festival of Harvest) is a time for thanksgiving, meditation, and introspection. On this sacred day, Witches rededicate themselves to the Craft, and Wiccan initiation ceremonies are performed by the High Priestesses and Priests of covens. Many Wiccan traditions also perform a special rite for the goddess Persephone's descent into the Underworld as part of their Autumn Equinox celebration.

SEPTEMBER 23

On this date (approximately), the Sun enters the astrological sign of Libra. Persons born under the sign of the Scales (or Balance) are said to be artistic, resourceful, extroverted, balanced, and often indecisive. Libra is an air sign and is ruled by the planet Venus.

Libra

SEPTEMBER 24

In ancient Egypt, the annual death and rebirth of the god Osiris was celebrated once a year on this date. A festival held in his honor consisted of song, dance, and ceremonial plantings.

In West Africa, this day is sacred to Obatala, a hermaphrodite deity who was believed to have given birth to all Yoruban gods and goddesses.

SEPTEMBER 25

On this date in ancient Greece, a feast of beans known as the *Pyanopsia* was celebrated annually in honor of the great Olympian god Apollo and the three beautiful goddesses of the four seasons known as the Horae.

The birthday of Sedna, the Eskimo goddess of both the sea and the Underworld, is celebrated annually on this date in Greenland, northeastern Siberia, and the Arctic coastal regions of North America.

SEPTEMBER 26

Theseus, the great hero of Athens who slew the Minotaur and conquered the Amazons, was honored on this date in ancient Greece with an annual festival called the *Theseia*. The celebration lasted until the twenty-ninth day of September.

In ancient times, a goat sacrifice was performed annually on this day to appease Azazel, a Hebrew fallen angel who seduced mankind. He was associated with the planet Mars.

SEPTEMBER 27

Moon Festival. On this date, an annual ceremony takes place in China to honor the Moon Hare and to give thanks to the gods for a harvest of abundance. The rites associated with the Moon Festival are always performed by women as the Moon represents yin, the female cosmic element.

SEPTEMBER 28

On this date in ancient Athens, an annual *Thesmophoria* festival was celebrated in honor of the Greek goddess Demeter. The festival lasted until the third day of October.

SEPTEMBER 29

Michaelmas. According to English folklore, it was on this day that the Devil fell from Heaven, landed on a blackberry bush, and cursed the berries. Therefore, it is unlucky to pick blackberries after Michaelmas. In parts of Scotland, special Michaelmas cakes are eaten by the superstitious on this day to ward off all evil and misfortune in the coming year.

SEPTEMBER 30

On this date, the annual *Meditrinalia* festival was celebrated in the city of Rome in honor of the goddess Meditrina, a deity who presided over medicines and the arts of healing.

In ancient Greece, the *Epitaphia* was held once a year on this date to honor the souls of warriors slain in battle.

OCTOBER

OCTOBER, the tenth month of the current Gregorian calendar and the second month of Autumn's rule, derives its name from octo, the Latin word meaning "eight," as October was the eighth month of the old Roman calendar.

The traditional birthstone amulets of October are opal, rose sapphire, and tourmaline; and the calendula is the month's traditional flower.

October is shared by the astrological signs of Libra the Scales (or Balance) and Scorpio the Scorpion, and is sacred to the following Pagan deities: Cernunnos, Hecate, the Morrigan, Osiris, and the Wiccan Goddess in Her dark aspect as the Crone.

During the month of October, the Great Solar Wheel of the Year is turned to Halloween (Samhain Eve), one of the four Grand Sabbats celebrated each year by Wiccans and modern Witches throughout the world.

OCTOBER 1

On this date (approximately), hundreds of thousands of Muslims make a pilgrimage to the city of Mecca to kiss and touch the Black Stone (one of the original building blocks of a veiled shrine) and to worship their god Allah. They then drink some water from the nearby sacred Well of Ishmael, and journey up into the hills of Safa and Marwa to recite prayers.

OCTOBER 2

Guiding Spirits Day. On this day, light a white candle on your altar and give thanks to your spirit guide (or guides) for guarding over you and guiding you through your spiritual development. If you wish to communicate with or meet your spirit guide, use a Ouija board or, through prayer, invite the spirit guide to come to you in a dream or in a trance.

OCTOBER 3

On this date (approximately), a Cementation and Propitiation Festival was once celebrated by the Native American tribe of the Cherokee. The purpose of the festival was to remove the barriers between the Cherokee people and the deities they worshiped.

OCTOBER 4

On this date in ancient Rome, a day of fasting known as the *Jejunium Cereris* was observed in honor of Ceres (Mother Earth), the corn-goddess and protectress of agriculture and all fruits of the Earth.

OCTOBER 5

The Festival of the Old Woman (*Nubaigai*) is celebrated annually on this date by farm workers in Lithuania. The last sheaf of grain is dressed up as a woman and a festival of feasting, merriment, and games is held to honor the goddess of the corn.

In the country of Rumania, the *Dionysiad* wine festival was held annually on this date in honor of Dionysus, Ariadne, and the Maenads.

OCTOBER 6

On this date, an annual nine-day religious festival begins in Nepal to honor the great Hindu god Vishnu and to celebrate his awakening on a bed of serpents. As part of an ancient tradition, secret offerings are made to the god and placed in unripe pumpkins.

OCTOBER 7

In the fifteenth century, peasants in Germany celebrated a weeklong festival called the *Kermesse*. A Pagan icon (or some other sacred object) would be unearthed from its yearlong burial spot and then paraded through the village on top of a gaily decorated pole. After a week of feasting, dancing, and games, the villagers would dress up in their mourning attire and rebury the icon in its grave, where it would remain until the next year's *Kermesse*.

On this date in the year 1909, famous author and Gardnerian Witch Arnold Crowther was born in Kent, England. He was initiated into the Craft in 1960 by Patricia Dawson, whom he later married. He passed away on Beltane Sabbat in the year 1974.

OCTOBER 8

On this day, an annual good luck festival called *Chung Yeung Day* (the Festival of High Places) is celebrated in China. Traditionally good omen kites are flown to carry away evil spirits.

The festival also commemorates an ancient Chinese scholar names Huan Ching who, upon heeding the warning of a soothsayer, escaped with his family and friends high into the hills and thereby avoided a mysterious plague of death which swept through the village below, killing every living thing in sight.

OCTOBER 9

Day of Felicitas. A festival celebrating the ancient Roman goddess of luck and good fortune was held annually on this date in many parts of Italy. For many Wiccans and modern Witches, it is a time for casting spells and making amulets to attract good luck or to end a streak of bad luck.

OCTOBER 10

Throughout the country of Brazil, the annual Festival of Light begins on this date. The centuries-old festival, which is celebrated for two consecutive weeks, includes a parade of penance and the lighting of candles, torches, and hearth-fires to symbolically drive away the spirits of darkness who bring evil and misfortune.

OCTOBER 11

Every year on this date, Witches in the countries of Denmark and Germany honor the Old Lady of the Elder Trees, an ancient Pagan spirit who dwells within and watches over each and every tree of the elder family. Before cutting any branches to use as magick wands, a libation of elderberry wine is poured onto the tree's roots and a special prayer is recited.

OCTOBER 12

On this date in the year 1875, famous occultist and ceremonial magician Aleister Crowley was born in Warwickshire,

England. He authored many popular and controversial books on the subject of magick, and was notorious for his rites of sex magick, ceremonial sorcery, and blood sacrifices. Crowley often referred to himself as the Beast of the Apocalypse and was nicknamed The Wickedest Man in the World by the news media and by many who knew him personally. He died on December 1, 1947, and after his cremation, his ashes were shipped to his followers in the United States of America.

Also on this date in the year 1888, famous ceremonial magician and occult author Eliphas Levi died.

OCTOBER 13

On this date in the year 1917, the Goddess in the guise of the Virgin Mary made her final visit (as promised earlier that year) to three children in the Portuguese town of Fatima. She revealed many predictions to the children, and a crowd of over 70,000 pilgrims who gathered for the miraculous event witnessed a strange object—resembling a huge silver disk blazing with colored flames—fly through the sky.

OCTOBER 14

Each year on this date, the planets of the Milky Way galaxy are honored and celebrated by an event known as Interplanetary Confederation Day.

In Bangladesh, an annual festival called *Durga Puja* is celebrated on this day to commemorate the great Mother-Goddess Durga and her triumph over the forces of evil.

OCTOBER 15

On this date in ancient Rome, a sacred harvest festival dedicated to the god Mars was celebrated with a chariot race, followed by the sacrifice of the slowest horse. (Before becoming a god of battle, Mars was originally a deity associated with fertility and agriculture.)

OCTOBER 16

Each year on this date, the Festival of the Goddess of Fortune (*Lakshmi Puji*) is celebrated in Nepal. The goddess Lakshmi is honored with prayers, sacred chants, and offerings of flower petals and fragrant incense.

OCTOBER 17

Once a year on this date, the Japanese Shinto ceremony of *Kanname-Sai* (God Tasting Event) takes place. The ancient goddess of the Sun and other imperial ancestors are honored with an offering of rice from the season's first crop.

OCTOBER 18

In England, the Great Horned Fair takes place annually on this day to celebrate the wondrous powers of nature and fertility. Many Pagans and Wiccans (especially of the Gardnerian tradition) perform a special ceremony on this day in honor of Cernunnos, the Horned God of hunting, fertility, and wild animals. He is also the consort of the Goddess, and a symbol of the male principle. At this time, many priests of Wiccan covens perform a sacred ritual called Drawing Down the Sun.

OCTOBER 19

On this day, an annual fair called *Bettara-Ichi* ("Sticky-Sticky Fair") is held in Tokyo, Japan near the sacred shrine of the god Ebisu. Children carry sticky pickled radishes tied to straw ropes through the streets in order to chase away evil spirits and to receive blessings from the seven Shinto gods of good luck.

OCTOBER 20

On this date in the year 1949, Wiccan priestess and spiritual healer Selena Fox was born in Arlington, Virginia. In 1974, with the help of Jim Alan and a small group of Neo-Pagan friends, she formed Circle Sanctuary in Wisconsin. She is known as one of the leading religious-freedom activists in the Wiccan and Neo-Pagan movements.

OCTOBER 21

In the former Czechoslovakia, an annual festival known as the Day of Ursala is held on this date in honor of Ursala, the ancient lunar goddess of Slavic mythology who later became Saint Ursala.

OCTOBER 22

In Japan, the purifying Festival of Fire (*Hi Matsuri*) is celebrated annually on this night. A traditional torchlight procession parades through the streets of Kurama and ends at a sacred shrine, where the ancient gods are believed to return to Earth at the stroke of midnight.

OCTOBER 23

On this date (approximately), the Sun enters the astrological sign of Scorpio. Persons born under the sign of the Scorpion are said to be magnetic, psychic, imaginative, mysterious, and often prone to jealous obsessions. Scorpio is a water sign and is ruled by the planets Mars and Pluto.

Scorpio

OCTOBER 24

On this day, many Wiccans from around the world celebrate the annual Feast of the Spirits of Air. Incense is offered up to the Sylphs (who often take the form of butterflies), and rituals involving dreams and/or the powers of the mind are performed.

This day is sacred to Arianrhod, Cardea, Dione, Diti, Gula, Lilith, Maat, Minerva, and Sophia.

OCTOBER 25

Shoemaker's Day is celebrated annually on this date in honor of Saint Crispin, the patron of shoemakers who was beheaded in the third century A.D. According to legend, a new pair of shoes bought on this day will bring good luck and prosperity to their owner.

OCTOBER 26

Birthday of the Earth. According to the calculations of a seventeenth-century Anglican archbishop, the Earth was created on this date in the year 4004 B.C.

On this date in the year 1440, Giles de Rais (one of the most notorious necromancers in history) was hanged in

France as punishment for practicing black magick and making human sacrifices to the Devil, among other crimes.

OCTOBER 27

Allan Apple Day. In Cornwall, England, an old Pagan method of love divination is traditionally performed each year on this day. A single gentleman or lady who wishes to see his or her future spouse must sleep with an Allan apple under his or her pillow, then get out of bed before the crack of dawn the next day. The person then waits under a tree for the first person of the opposite sex to walk by. According to the legend, the passerby will be the future marriage mate.

OCTOBER 28

In ancient times, the Phoenician sun-god Baal of the Heavens was honored annually on or around this date. He presided over nature and fertility, and was associated with winter rain. Sacred sun-symbolizing bonfires were lit in his honor by his worshipers in Syria. Depicted as a warrior with a horned helmet and spear, he was once worshiped as the principal god on Earth for thousands of years.

In ancient Egypt, a series of Autumn ceremonies for the goddess Isis began each year on this date. They lasted for six consecutive days.

OCTOBER 29

On this date in the year 1939, ceremonial magician and occult author Frater Zarathustra was born in Baltimore, Maryland. Frater founded the Temple of Truth in 1972 and was publisher and editor of the *White Light* (a magazine of ceremonial magick) from 1973 until it ceased publication in 1990.

On this day, the Native American tribe of the Iroquois celebrate their annual Feast of the Dead to honor the souls of departed loved ones.

OCTOBER 30

Each year on this date, the *Angelitos* festival is held in Mexico to bless the souls of deceased children and to honor Xipe Totec (the ancient god of death) and Tonantzin (the Guadualupe goddess of mercy).

On this day, write a secret wish on a piece of dried mandrake root. Burn it at the stroke of midnight in a fireproof container and then go outside and cast the ashes to the wind as you say thrice: "Spirits of fire, spirits of air; grant this secret wishing-prayer. Let the ashes of this spell, fix this midnight magick well."

OCTOBER 31

Halloween (also known as Samhain Eve, Hallowmas, All Hallow's Eve, All Saint's Eve, Festival of the Dead, and the Third Festival of Harvest).

Every year on this day, the most important of the eight Witches' Sabbats is celebrated by Wiccans throughout the world with traditional Pagan feasts, bonfires, and rituals to honor the spirits of deceased loved ones. The divinatory arts of scrying and rune-casting are traditionally practiced by Wiccans on this magickal night, as is standing before a mirror and making a secret wish.

The last night of October was the ancient Celt's New Year's Eve. It marked the end of the Summer and the beginning of Winter (also known as the dark half of the year).

In many parts of the world, special cakes and food are prepared for the dead on this night.

In Ireland, a Halloween festival is celebrated annually for the ancient Pagan goddess Tara.

This day is sacred to the goddesses Cerridwen, Eurydice, Hecate, Hel, Inanna, Kali, the Morrigan, Nephthys, Oya, Samia, Sedna, Tara, and Vanadis. On this day in the year 1970, the Parks Department of New York City granted the Witches International Craft Associates (W.I.C.A.) a permit to hold a "Witch-in." The event was held in Sheep Meadow and more than one thousand persons attended.

(Abraham Saur, *Ein Kurtze Treue Warning*, 1582)

NOVEMBER

NOVEMBER, the eleventh month of the current Gregorian calendar and the third month of Autumn's rule, derives its name from *novem*, the Latin word meaning "nine," as November was the ninth month of the old Roman Calendar.

The traditional birthstone amulet of November is the topaz; and the chrysanthemum is the month's traditional flower.

November is shared by the astrological signs of Scorpio the Scorpion and Sagittarius the Centaur-Archer, and is sacred to the following Pagan deities: Astarte, Calleach, Hathor, Kali, Maman, and Sekhmet.

NOVEMBER 1

On this day in ancient Rome, the harvest-goddess of fruit trees, orchards, and all fruit-bearing plants was honored with a festival called the *Pomonia* (Feast of Pomona) which marked the end of the growing season.

Many modern Witches celebrate the day after the Halloween Sabbat with a feast commemorating fruition, maturity, immortality, and resurrection.

All Saints' Day. This is one of the most magickal and powerful days of the year to practitioners of Voodoo, and a time to perform rituals for spiritual strength and protection against evil loas (spirit-gods).

In Latin America and Spain, the Day of the Dead is celebrated on this date with offerings of food to honor the spirits of deceased loved ones.

A festival known as Cailleach's Reign is celebrated annually on this date by many Pagans throughout Ireland and Great Britain in honor of the ancient Celtic Crone-Goddess.

NOVEMBER 2

All Souls' Day. In England, small offerings known as soul cakes are traditionally set out for the dead every year on this date.

According to folklore, this is considered to be an extremely unlucky day for wedding ceremonies. Those who are wed on All Souls' Day are sure to be cursed with misfortune, illness, divorce, or an early death.

NOVEMBER 3

On this date in the year 1324, a Witch named Dame Alice Kyteler suffered death by fire in the first and most famous

Witch trial to take place in Ireland. Nine others were arrested, found guilty, and sentenced to various punishments.

In Egypt, the final day of the *Isia* takes place on this day. This annual festival celebrates the rebirth of the god Osiris through the sacred and life-giving milk of Isis.

NOVEMBER 4

In ancient times, a Pagan festival honoring the Lord of Death was celebrated in England every year on this night (the Eve of Guy Fawkes Day). The bonfires and mischievous pranks associated with modern England's Mischief Night are actually remnants of the old Pagan customs.

NOVEMBER 5

Every year on this date, young men gather in Shebbear, England, to turn a large red rock called the Devil's Boulder. The centuries-old custom of turning the one-ton rock (which was flung into the village square by the Devil himself, according to English folklore) conjures up ancient magickal powers and brings peace and prosperity to the village.

NOVEMBER 6

On this day, the birth of Tiamat (an ancient Babylonian goddess known as the Dragon Mother) is celebrated. According to mythology, Tiamat and her consort Apsu gave birth to all the gods of the world, and the earth and the heavens were created from Dragon Mother's severed body.

NOVEMBER 7

Night of Hecate. In ancient Greece, a fire festival was held once a year on this night to honor the goddess Hecate.

Modern Witches invoke Hecate for protection and fertility, as she is both a protectress of all Witches and an ancient deity associated with fertility.

In the Hawaiian Islands, the ancient god Lono is honored annually on this day by the Hawaiian Harvest Festival. The *Makahiki* festival also takes place in Hawaii on this day.

NOVEMBER 8

In Haiti, farmers make offerings of yams to their family's ancestral spirits and household gods every year on this day (approximately) in order to insure a bountiful harvest in the next year.

Hettsui No Kami, the kitchen-range goddess, is honored on this day in Japan with an annual Shinto festival called the *Fuigo Matsuri.*

NOVEMBER 9

In Thailand, a traditional wish-magick ritual is performed annually on this date. Banana peels and lotus leaves are made into little boats and filled with candles and various offerings to the gods (such as incense, coins, and gardenia flowers). Secret wishes are made as the "boats" are set adrift on a river, and if the candles keep burning until they are out of view, the wishes are said to come true.

NOVEMBER 10

On this date in olden times, Old November Eve was celebrated throughout the Scottish countryside. The goddess Nicnevin was honored with prayers and feasts, and it was believed that she rode through the air and made herself visible to mortals on this night.

On this date (approximately) in the year 1493, famous

Hermetic philosopher and alchemist Paracelsus was born in Einsiedeln, Switzerland. (However, other sources give his date of birth as December 17, 1493.) Paracelsus possessed remarkable healing powers and believed in a universal natural magick. Contrary to many writings about him, he was not a sorcerer or a practitioner of ceremonial magick (in fact, he was known to be rather skeptical of the so-called Black Arts); however, he did believe in astrology and often used magickal astrological talismans (inscribed with planetary symbols) in his medical practice. He died a mysterious death in Salzburg in the year 1541.

Paracelsus

NOVEMBER 11
Old November Day

In Ireland, the Faerie Sidhe is honored on this day with an annual Pagan festival known as the *Lunantshees*.

A festival called The Day of the Heroes is celebrated annually on this day by Pagans and Wiccans in northern Europe. The ancient deities of the Norse mythos are honored with prayers and merry feasts.

On this day, the annual feast of *Vinalia* was observed by the ancient Greeks in honor of the wine-god Bacchus.

NOVEMBER 12

An annual festival called the *Epulum Jovis in Capitola* was celebrated on this date in ancient times in honor of Jupiter (the supreme god of the ancient Roman religion, identified with the Greek god Zeus) and the goddesses Minerva and Juno. Animal sacrifices were made at temples in the city of Rome and bonfires were set ablaze at sunset.

NOVEMBER 13

Back in medieval times, the thirteenth day after the Witches' Sabbat of Halloween was considered a day of darkness, evil, and misfortune. It was believed to be a time when necromancers and sorcerers of the left-hand path summoned up evil spirits and demons to assist them in their practice of the Black Arts.

In some parts of the world, the old superstition persists that if the thirteenth day after Halloween falls on a Friday, all persons born on that day will possess the power of the evil eye.

NOVEMBER 14

On this date, an annual Druidic festival known as the Feast of the Musicians is celebrated by many Wiccans to honor the ancient Celtic gods of music. Traditional Pagan folk songs are sung around an open fire as various offerings are cast into the flames.

At temples throughout India, children gather annually on this day to receive divine blessings from the Children's Goddesses: Befana, Mayauel, Rumina, and Surabhi.

NOVEMBER 15

Ferona, an ancient goddess who presides over fire, fertility, and woodlands, is honored annually on this day with a Pagan festival called the *Feronia*.

In Japan, a centuries-old ritual for good health (*Shichi-Go-San*) is performed annually on this date in Shinto shrines. The ceremony involves children who have reached the ages of three, five, and seven. At the end, the children are given candy blessed and decorated with symbols of good fortune.

On this date in the year 1280, German alchemist and ceremonial magician Albertus Magnus died. According to legend, he discovered the Philosopher's Stone and also created a supernatural zombie-like servant using natural magick and astrological science.

NOVEMBER 16

On this date (approximately), the annual Festival of Lights is celebrated in India to mark the Hindu New Year. Candles are lit to honor Lakshmi (the goddess who presides over wealth, prosperity, and sexual pleasures), and homes are decorated with ancient good-fortune ritual designs called *kolams*.

NOVEMBER 17

The last of three annual festivals of death is observed in certain regions of China on this day (approximately). Paper clothing and money labeled with the names of the dead are traditionally burned as offerings to ancestors in the spirit world.

On this date in the year 1907, famous occultist and author Israel Regardie was born in England. He belonged to the Hermetic Order of the Golden Dawn, and was a onetime secretary of Aleister Crowley. He wrote numerous books which continue to be popular among Witches, Neo-Pagans, and practitioners of the occult arts. Regardie died in the year 1983.

NOVEMBER 18

Ardvi, a Persian goddess believed to be the Mother of the Stars, is honored annually on this date with a sacred festival called the *Ardvi Sura* (The Day of Ardvi). The festival, which takes place under the nighttime stars, has been celebrated by the faithful in southwestern Asia since ancient times.

NOVEMBER 19

Warlock Day. According to medieval superstitious belief, the first stranger you meet on this day who is dressed in black from head to toe will be a warlock (a male Witch). Take care not to look him directly in the eyes; otherwise, you will become bewitched.

NOVEMBER 20

On this night, when the Pleiades (a cluster of stars in the constellation of Taurus) become visible to the naked eye, native rituals and celebrations begin in Hawaii to mark the beginning of their harvest season and to honor and give thanks to the ancient god Lono.

NOVEMBER 21

In ancient times, a joyous Mayan festival honoring the god Kukulcan began each year on this date. The celebration lasted for several days and nights.

This day is also sacred to the Pagan gods Chango, Damballah, Quetzalcoatl, and Tammuz.

NOVEMBER 22

On this date (approximately), the Sun enters the astrological sign of Sagittarius. Persons born under the sign of the Centaur-Archer are said to be optimistic, enthusiastic, curious, and often outspoken and prone to exaggeration. Sagittarius is a fire sign and is ruled by the planet Jupiter.

Sagittarius

NOVEMBER 23

On this day in England, Saint Clement (the patron of ironworkers) is honored with elaborate rituals. However, in ancient times, this day was celebrated with a Pagan feast in honor of the wizard-blacksmith of the Saxon deities.

In Japan, a rice harvest celebration called the Shinjosai Festival for Konohana-Hime is held yearly on this date. It is dedicated to the granddaughter goddess of the solar deity Amaterasu.

NOVEMBER 24

In Japan, the annual festival known as *Tori-No-Ichi* takes place on or around this date. Traditionally, special bamboo rakes decorated with symbols of good fortune are carried through the streets in order to attract benevolent spirits.

In ancient Egypt, the sacred goddesses of light and birth were honored and invoked annually on or around this day with prayers, libations, and the ritual burning of special lamps.

NOVEMBER 25

Windmill Blessing Day. In days of old, many millers in Holland would bless their windmills on or around this date each year by throwing a handful or two of flour into the wind as an offering to appease the mischievous invisible entities known as the Windmill Spirits.

NOVEMBER 26

On this date (approximately), annual manhood initiation rites are performed by young males in the Basari villages of Senegal. The centuries-old ceremonies are followed by a joyous celebration of dancing, singing, and athletic competition.

A centuries-old fire festival takes place every year on this day in Tibet. The festival is dedicated to the ancient goddesses who rule over light and fire.

NOVEMBER 27

The Indian Mother-Goddess known as Gujeswari is honored on or around this date each year by Buddhists and Hindus in Nepal. Prayers are recited throughout the day, and a musical procession fills the streets with sacred songs after sunset.

In India, a religious festival called the *Parvati-Devi* takes place on this day each year. It honors the triple goddess known as the Mother of the Universe, whose three goddess aspects are Sarasvati (Maiden), Lakshmi (Mother), and Parvati (Crone).

NOVEMBER 28

Sophia, the ancient Greek goddess of wisdom and inner truth, is honored and invoked annually on this day by chants, libations, and secret Pagan rituals performed by those who seek to acquire arcane knowledge.

NOVEMBER 29

Each year on this night (according to ancient legend), vampires in Rumania are believed to rise up from their graves after a yearlong sleep and walk the Earth in search of human blood. Garlic and crucifixes are hung on doors and windows for protection.

In ancient Egypt, the Feast of Hathor as Sekhmet was held each year on this day. It honored the lion-headed goddess of battle, who was also the consort of the moon-god Ptah.

NOVEMBER 30
Saint Andrew's Night

In many rural villages in Germany, young women still perform traditional love-divinations on this night. Using various methods of fortune-telling, they read omens and dreams to find out about their future husbands and marriages.

On this date in the year 1942, Otter Zell (Pagan priest and the founder of The Church of All Worlds) was born in Saint Louis, Missouri.

DECEMBER

DECEMBER, the twelfth and final month of the current Gregorian calendar and the first month of Winter, derives its name from decem, the Latin word meaning "ten," as December was the tenth month of the old Roman calendar.

The traditional birthstone amulets of December are the blue zircon and turquoise; and holly, mistletoe, and poinsettia are the month's traditional flowers.

December is shared by the astrological signs of Sagittarius the Centaur-Archer and Capricorn the Goat, and is sacred to the following Pagan deities: Attis, Dionysus, Frey, Freya (or Freyja), Kriss Kringle (the Pagan god of Yule), Lucina, Woden, and the Wiccan Horned God (consort of the Wiccan Goddess).

During the month of December, the Great Solar Wheel of the Year is turned to the Winter Solstice, one of the four Lesser Sabbats celebrated each year by Wiccans and modern Witches throughout the world.

DECEMBER 1

In some parts of the world, the first day of December is the traditional time for young girls to perform the ancient art of cromniomancy (divination by onion sprouts) to find out the name of their future husbands.

To find out who your future husband will be, take some onions and upon each one carve or write a different man's name. Place the onions near a fire and the man whose name is on the onion that sprouts first will be the one.

DECEMBER 2

In what is now known as Bodh Gaya, India, the world's oldest and most sacred tree (planted in the year 282 B.C. and believed to be an offshoot of the Bodhi or Bo-tree that the Buddha sat under when he achieved enlightenment) is honored annually on this date by Tibetan Buddhist pilgrims with prayers, chants, and brightly colored flags.

On this day, an annual women's festival called *Hari Kugo* (Broken Needles) takes place in the city of Tokyo. It commemorates women's crafts and is dedicated to all patron goddesses of Japanese craftswomen.

DECEMBER 3

In ancient Rome, secret women's rites were performed annually on this date in honor of Bona Dea, the Good Goddess. All males were barred from the ceremonies, which were conducted by vestal virgins.

In ancient Greece, this day was sacred to the goddess Cybele and also to Rhea, the Great Mother of the Earth.

DECEMBER 4

On this date in ancient Rome, the goddess Minerva was honored with an annual festival. Minerva (the Roman counterpart of the Greek Athena) is a goddess of battle and also a patroness of the arts and wisdom.

In West Africa, this day is sacred to the Yoruban god Chango. He is a god of lightning bolts, and the son of the deities Yemaya and Orungan.

DECEMBER 5

In ancient Greece, an annual seaside festival (the *Poseidea*) was celebrated annually on this date to honor the sea-god Poseidon, consort of the Mother Goddess.

In Italy, the First Feast of Saint Lucia is held on this date each year. Before being Christianized into a Saint, she was originally worshiped as Lucina, a Pagan goddess of light who also presided over childbirth.

DECEMBER 6

On this day in the year 1890, famous occultist and ritual magician Dion Fortune was born in Wales. Although Ms. Fortune never proclaimed herself to be a Witch, her numerous writings are popular among (and inspiring to) many modern Witches, Wiccans, and Neo-Pagans around the world. She died from leukemia on January 8, 1946.

DECEMBER 7

On this date in ancient Greece, an annual rite called the Haloia of Demeter was performed. According to mythology, each year the goddess Demeter wanders the earth in search of her stolen daughter Persephone. The goddess' sorrow brings Winter to the world and all trees and flowers cease to bloom; however, Spring returns when Persephone is allowed to temporarily leave the darkness of the Underworld and Demeter once again rejoices.

DECEMBER 8

On this day, the birth of the ancient and powerful goddess of the sun (Amaterasu) is celebrated annually at Shinto temples throughout Japan.

In Egypt, the Festival of Neith is celebrated annually on this date to honor the Earth-Goddess of the Delta.

DECEMBER 9

The ninth day of the last month of the year (along with the sixth and seventh days) is considered to be an extremely unlucky time, according to Grafton in his *Manuel* (a sixteenth-century book of unlucky days as determined by professional star-gazers).

In Mexico, the healing virgin-goddess Tonantzin is honored on this day with an annual festival called the Fiesta of the Mother of Health.

DECEMBER 10

On this night (approximately), Inuit hunters in the far north begin an annual five-day series of purification rites, followed by a propitiation ceremony under the full moon, for the souls of the animals they had hunted in the last year. The December Moon ceremony has been performed in the Arctic coastal regions of North America for hundreds of years.

DECEMBER 11

Day of Bruma. On this date, the ancient Roman goddess of the winter season was honored by Pagans in Italy with an annual festival.

This day is also sacred to Arianrhod, the Snow Queen goddess, and Yuki Onne.

DECEMBER 12

The victories of good over evil and light over darkness are celebrated annually at sunset on this date (approximately) with the Zoroastrian fire festival of Sada.

In Mexico, the annual Our Lady of Guadalupe religious festival takes place on this day. It is a sacred day to the goddesses Coatlique, Tonantzin, and the Black Madonna.

DECEMBER 13

Saint Lucia's Day. On this day, a candlelight festival is celebrated throughout Sweden. The first-born daughter of each family wears a flowing white gown and a crown of candles around her head, obviously in reference to the ancient Pagan symbols of fire and life-giving light. The daughter traditionally serves her mother and father breakfast in bed.

DECEMBER 14

On this date in the year 1503, the famous French prophet and astrologer Michel de Nostradamus was born in Saint Remy de Provence. He experienced many psychic visions during his childhood, and he later studied the Holy Qabalah, astrology, astronomy, medicine, and mathematics. The first collection of his uncannily accurate visions, written in the form of rhymed quatrains, was published in the year 1555. Three years later, a second and larger collection of his prophecies—reaching into the year 3797—was published. Nostradamus died on July 1, 1566.

Nostradamus

DECEMBER 15

Halcyon Days. According to ancient legend, the seven days before the winter solstice and the seven days following it are a special time of tranquility and calm, due to the magickal powers of the halcyon (a fabled bird who nested on the sea and calmed the wind and the waves during the winter solstice).

In Puerto Rico, the Yule Child is honored by a religious festival called *Navidades*, which begins annually on this day. It is celebrated until the sixth of January.

DECEMBER 16

In Mexico, the Yule Child is honored by a religious festival called *Posadas*, which begins annually on this day. It is celebrated until the twenty-fourth of December.

This day is sacred to the Pagan wisdom-goddesses Athena, Kista, Maat, Minerva, the Shekinah, and Sophia.

The *Soyal* ceremony is celebrated annually on this date (approximately) by the Native American tribe of the Hopi in the southwestern United States. The rites of the *Soyal* celebrate the return of the sun (Life) and commemorate the creation and rebirth of Spider Woman and Hawk Maiden.

DECEMBER 17

Saturnalia. The Roman god Saturn was honored in ancient times during this annual midwinter festival, which began on this date and lasted until the twenty-fourth of December. This was a week of feasting, merriment, gift-giving, charades, and the lighting of torches and candles.

DECEMBER 18

On this day in Latvia, the birth of the god Diev and the rebirth of the Sun is celebrated annually with a four-day winter festival. Houses are festively decorated and traditional feasts are prepared to welcome the four gift-bearing celestial beings who are the heralds of the winter solstice.

On the second day of the *Saturnalia,* the ancient Romans celebrated the *Eponalia* (a feast dedicated to Epona, the Celtic Mother-Goddess and a patroness of horses).

DECEMBER 19

On the third day of the *Saturnalia,* the ancient Romans celebrated the *Opalia,* a feast dedicated to Ops (Abundance), the harvest goddess of fertility and success, and the consort of the god Saturn. This day was also sacred to the Roman fertility goddess Sabine.

The Hindu goddess Sankrant is honored annually on this date (approximately) by a Hindu Solstice celebration called *Pongol.*

DECEMBER 20

On this day in the year 1946, famous Israeli psychic Uri Geller was born in Tel Aviv. He is renowned for his psychokinetic ability to bend metal objects by stroking them with his fingers and to stop clocks simply by gazing upon them. His metal-bending and mind-reading abilities developed at the age of five when he was accidentally shocked by his mother's electric sewing machine. He began his career as a full-time professional stage performer in 1969.

DECEMBER 21

On the first day of winter (which normally occurs on or near this date), the Winter Solstice Sabbat is celebrated by Wiccans and Witches throughout the world. Winter Solstice (which is also known as Yule, Winter Rite, Midwinter, and Alban Arthan) is the longest night of the year, marking the time when the days begin to grow longer and the hours of darkness decrease. It is the festival of the Sun's rebirth, and a time to honor the Horned God. (The aspect of the God invoked at this Sabbat by certain Wiccan traditions is Frey, the Scandinavian fertility god and a deity associated with peace and prosperity.) Love, family togetherness, and accomplishments of the past year are also celebrated. On this Sabbat, Witches bid farewell to the Great Mother and welcome the reborn Horned God who rules the dark half of the year.

DECEMBER 22

On this date (approximately), the Sun enters the astrological sign of Capricorn. Persons born under the sign of the Goat are said to be ambitious, practical, loyal, and often reclusive. Capricorn is an earth sign and is ruled by the planet Saturn.

On this date in the year 1970, famous Wiccan authors Stewart and Janet Farrar founded their own coven. The Farrars, a husband and wife team, have written many popular Witchcraft books together.

Capricorn

DECEMBER 23

In early times, a Pagan religious ceremony called the *Laurentina* was held in Rome each year on this date. It celebrated the recovery of light from the darkness of the winter solstice, and was dedicated to the goddess Acca Laurentia or Lara (the mother of the Lares).

The demigod Balomain is honored annually by the Kalash people with a weeklong festival called the *Chaomos,* which begins on this date.

DECEMBER 24

Christmas Eve. According to Finnish folklore, the ghosts of departed loved ones return home each year on this night. It is a Christmas Eve tradition in Finland and in many other parts of Europe for families to light white candles on the graves of their ancestors.

According to superstition, if a man proposes to his beloved on Christmas Eve and she accepts, they will surely enjoy a happy and love-filled marriage.

DECEMBER 25

Birthday of the Invincible Sun (*Dies Natalis Invicti Solis*). Before being Christianized as the Mass of Christ (Christmas), a festival honoring the god of the sun was celebrated on this day in ancient Rome. It was made a public holiday by the Emperor Aurelian in the year a.d. 272 and consisted of the lighting of sacred bonfires.

On Christmas Day, according to German folklore, a Yuletide Witch known as the *Lutzelfrau* flies through the sky on her broom, bringing mischief to mortals who fail to honor her with small presents. Another Yuletide Witch of German folklore is Perchta. In the southern regions of the country, it was an old Yuletide custom for children wearing masks and carrying besoms (Witch brooms) to go door to door (in "trick or treat" fashion) begging for gifts in the name of Perchta.

DECEMBER 26

On this day, the first day of Yuletide begins. It continues until the Twelfth-day (January 6).

The *Junkanoo* festival takes place annually on this day in the Bahama Islands. Old gods are honored and ancient magick is reinvoked as music, dancing, and costumed marchers fill the streets until the crack of dawn.

This day is sacred to various deities from around the world. Among them are Frau Sonne, Igaehindvo, the Star Faery, Sunne, and Yemaya.

DECEMBER 27

On this day in the year 1959, Gerina Dunwich (eclectic Witch, professional astrologer, and author of many Witchcraft books, including the one you are now reading) was born in Chicago, Illinois under the sign of Capricorn with a Taurus rising.

The birth of Freya (the Norse goddess of fertility, love, and beauty) is celebrated on this day. Annual Pagan festivals in her honor are celebrated throughout the world by many Wiccans of the Saxon tradition.

DECEMBER 28

On this day, an annual festival of peace and spiritual renewal is celebrated in parts of China. Offerings are made to gods and spirits, and a paper horse containing the names of all the members of the temple is set on fire in the ancient Taoist belief that the rising smoke will take the names up to heaven.

DECEMBER 29

During this period, the eight-day Jewish Festival of Lights (also known as Hanukkah or Chanukah) is observed by Jews throughout the world. On each night of the festival, one additional candle is lit on a ceremonial nine-branched candelabrum called a menorah.

In ancient Greece, a Pagan religious festival called The Day of Nymphs was celebrated on this day in honor of Andromeda, Ariadne, and Artemis (the Greek counterpart of the goddess Diana).

DECEMBER 30

On this date in the year 1916, Rasputin (a famous Russian mystic monk, occultist, and court magician) was assassinated by his enemy Prince Feliks Yusupov. Rasputin, who was drowned in the frozen Neva River, presaged his own death.

Rasputin

DECEMBER 31

New Year's Eve. The modern custom of ringing bells and blowing horns to usher in the new year at midnight is actually derived from the old Pagan custom of noisemaking to scare away the evils of the old year.

In certain parts of Japan, young men put on grotesque demon masks and costumes made of straw and go door to door collecting donations of money, rice cakes, and sake. This traditional New Year's Eve custom serves to drive out the demons of misfortune and ensure an abundant harvest for the new year.

BIBLIOGRAPHY

Bulfinch, Thomas. *Bulfinch's Mythology*, Dell Publishing Company, Inc., New York, NY, 1971. Fifth Printing.

Chapman, Colin. *Shadows of the Supernatural*, Lion Publishing, Oxford, England, 1990.

Croft, Peter. *All Color Book of Roman Mythology*, Chartwell Books, Inc., Secaucus, NJ, 1989 edition.

Encyclopedia of Witchcraft and Demonology (Introduction by Hans Holzer). Octopus Books, London, England, 1974.

Grebner, Bernice Prill. *The Day of Your Birth*, Grebner Books, Peoria Heights, IL, 1990.

Guiley, Rosemary Ellen. *The Encyclopedia of Witches and Witchcraft*, Facts on File, Inc., New York, NY, 1989.

___. *Harper's Encyclopedia of Mystical and Paranormal Experience*, Harper San Francisco, a division of HarperCollins Publishers, New York, NY, 1991.

Hamilton, Edith. *Mythology*, Little, Brown and Company, Boston, MA, 1942.

Hicks, Jim, series editor. *The Mystical Year (Mysteries of the Unknown)*, by the editors of Time-Life Books, Alexandria, Va, 1992.

Lyttelton, Margaret and Werner Forman. *The Romans: Their Gods and Their Beliefs*, Orbis Publishing Limited, London, England, 1984.

Pepper, Elizabeth and John Wilcox, executive editors. *The Witches' Almanac (Aries 1994–Pisces 1995)*, Pentacle Press, Milton, MA, 1994.

Perowne, Stewart. *Roman Mythology*, Hamlyn Publishing Group Limited, London, England, 1969.

Sansom, William. *A Book of Christmas*, McGraw-Hill Book Company, New York, NY, 1968.

Stein, Diane. *The Goddess Book of Days: A Perpetual 366 Day Engagement Calendar*, The Crossing Press, Freedom, CA, 1992. Second Edition.

Thompson, C.J.S. *The Hand of Destiny—Folklore and Superstition for Everyday Life*, Bell Publishing Company, New York, NY, 1989.

INDEX